Hot & Spicy
Latin Dishes

Also by Dave DeWitt, Mary Jane Wilan, and Melissa T. Stock

Hot & Spicy & Meatless

Hot & Spicy Chili

How to Order:
Single copies of this book may be ordered from Prima Publishing, P.O. Box 1260BK, Rocklin, CA 95677; telephone (916) 632-4400. Quantity discounts are also available. On your letterhead, include information concerning the intended use of the books and the number of books you wish to purchase.

Hot & Spicy Latin Dishes

Dave DeWitt

Mary Jane Wilan

Melissa T. Stock

Illustrations by Lois Bergthold

 Prima Publishing
P.O. Box 1260BK
Rocklin, CA 95677
(916) 632-4400

Portions of this book first appeared in *Chile Pepper* magazine. Used by permission.

Library of Congress Cataloging-in-Publication Data

DeWitt, Dave.
    Hot and spicy latin dishes : the best fiery foods from "Las Americas" / Dave De-Witt, Mary Jane Wilan, Melissa T. Stock.
       p.   cm.
    At head of title: Chile Pepper magazine presents.
    Includes index.
    ISBN 1-55958-484-X
    1. Cookery (Hot peppers)   2. Cookery, Latin American.   3. Hot peppers.
I. Wilan, Mary Jane.   I. Stock, Melissa T.   III. Chile pepper.   IV. Title.
TX803.P46D483 1994
641.6'384—dc20   94-30790
                                          CIP

96 97 98 99 **BB** 10 9 8 7 6 5 4 3 2

Printed in the United States of America

Acknowledgments

We'd like to thank the following people who helped us with this book: Jennifer Basye, Lois Bergthold, Louella Buchanan, Mary Dempsey, Alois Dogué, Winifred Galarza, Nancy Gerlach, Stuart Hutson, Tita Libín, José Marmolejo, David Parrish, Mark Preston, Loretta Salazar, Robert Spiegel, and David Tucker.

Contents

Introduction

Welcome to Latin America, the birthplace of chiles and—therefore—hot and spicy foods. Here the five major species of chiles evolved, were domesticated, and were adapted into some of the tastiest cuisines in the world. Although Mexico and parts of the Caribbean are also Latin, these regions have such a great variety of hot and spicy foods that they deserve separate treatment and will be the subjects of future books in this series.

South America is the center of origin for chiles, and in this book we refer to all five domesticated species. The species names are quite easy to follow, and here is a brief guide.

The pepper genus is *Capsicum,* from the Greek *kapto,* "to bite." The species are:

- *annuum,* meaning annual, which is an incorrect designation. It includes the most common varieties, such as New Mexican, jalapeño, bell, and wax.
- *baccatum,* meaning berry-like. It consists of the South American peppers commonly known as ajís.
- *chinense,* meaning from China, is also an incorrect designation. It includes the extremely hot habaneros.
- *frutescens,* meaning "shrubby" or "brushy." It includes the familiar tabascos.
- *pubescens,* meaning hairy. It includes the South American rocotos.

Remember that "ají" is both the generic term for the *baccatum* species and the generic South American term for all chiles of any species. Thus, it would not be unusual for a recipe entitled Ají de Gallina to contain rocoto chiles rather than ajís because, in the recipe title, the word is being used in its most general sense.

Although we were able to visit only a few of the many countries in Latin America, we have grown dozens of varieties of the chiles found there. One summer we grew fifteen varieties of the *chinense* species, including some extremely hot Brazilian pods. Another summer we raised twenty-two varieties of *baccatums* and used them in these recipes. Although the rocotos do not grow well in New Mexico, we have occasionally succeeded in producing a small crop of the thick-podded plants. We have also grown the malagueta chiles, those Latin relatives of tabascos.

This book is slightly ahead of its time because we call for the ajís and rocotos in some of our recipes, and they are relatively unavailable in North America. However, the seeds of these chiles are now available (see Mail Order Sources, p. 269), and many people are simply growing their own. We have suggested substitute chiles in each recipe, so that cooks can closely approximate the flavor and heat of the ajís and rocotos if they can't find them or grow them. Fortunately, the *annuum* varieties are commonly available fresh in North America, and habaneros have exploded onto the culinary scene and can be found fresh, dried, pickled, and concentrated into hot sauces.

Because certain countries in Latin America have hotter and spicier foods than others, it is not surprising that a great number of recipes in this book come from Peru and Brazil, where chiles are most beloved. But all of the other countries have delicious spicy foods too, and we have chosen the best dishes from Guatemala to Chile.

Latin America is notable for an enormous number of variations on a single dish as it appears in the cuisines of different countries. For example, we uncovered more than twenty-five different versions of ceviche and present our seven favorites. In other cases, we offer two or three different versions of other classic Latin dishes, such as stuffed chiles, matambre, and anticuchos. So, enjoy our hot and spicy tour!

For more coverage of Latin American and other hot and spicy cuisines, subscribe to *Chile Pepper* magazine, P.O. Box 80780, Albuquerque, NM 87198, (800) 359-1483.

1

El Nacimiento
The Birthplace of Hot & Spicy

Latin America, ancestral home of chile peppers, is an enigma when it comes to hot and spicy food. Since the fiery fruits originated there and proliferated for thousands of years before the Europeans arrived, we might assume that the prevalence of chiles had caused hot and spicy dishes to permeate all of the cuisines of this vast region. But in Central and South America, countries such as Brazil and Peru feature especially hot dishes while Costa Rica, Venezuela, and Argentina do not.

In the countries where European influences had a great impact upon the cuisines, the food tends to be milder. The pockets of heat are the spicier countries where the indigenous Native American population had a greater effect on the cuisine than did the European settlers. And with the exception of Brazil, which had African influences, these pockets are the regions where the great civilizations of the Maya, Aztec, and Inca arose:

Yucatán in Central America, the Valley of Mexico, Peru, and nearby Andean countries.

Andean Heat

The country people of the Andean regions of Peru, Chile, Ecuador, and Bolivia still eat basically Incan food that has been only slightly modified by the meats and vegetables introduced by the Spanish. But despite the basic nature of the cuisine of this region, chiles are used extensively, and they are among the hottest in the world.

Although the habanero relatives of the *chinense* species of the *Capsicum* genus do occasionally appear in the Andes, the two major chiles of choice in the region are ajís and rocotos. The *baccatum* species, familiarly termed "ají" throughout South America, originated either in Bolivia or in Peru and, according to archaeological evidence, was probably domesticated in Peru around 2,500 B.C.

Extensive *baccatum* material found at the Huaca Prieta archaeological site shows that the species was gradually improved by the pre-Incan civilizations. From tiny, berry-like pods that were deciduous (dropped off the plant), the fruit size increased, and the fruits gradually became non-deciduous and stayed on the plant through ripening. There are two wild forms (varieties *baccatum* and *microcarpum*) and a domesticated form (variety *pendulum*). The domesticated form has a great diversity of pod shape and size, ranging from short, pointed pods borne erect to long, pendant pods resembling the New Mexican varieties of the *annuum* species. The *baccatum* species is generally distinguished from the other species by the yellow or tan spots on the corollas of the flowers. One variety of ají, *puca-uchu*, grows on a vinelike plant in home gardens. *Baccatums* are cultivated in Argentina, Colombia, Ecuador, Peru, Brazil, and Bolivia. They are used fresh in salsas, and the small yellow varieties are prized for their lemony aroma. The pods of all ajís are also dried in the sun and then crushed into powders.

Writing in *Chile Pepper,* Mary Dempsey noted: "Ají is a banana pepper-shaped pepper called 'ají amarillo' when it is yellow or orange and 'ají colorado' when red—a distinction that is important only in the hue of the dish being prepared. When dried, it is often referred to as 'cuzqueño,' after the city of Cuzco. Piles of the orange, gold, and brilliant red peppers are found in every outdoor market in Peru, tossed in jumbled piles, stacked in pyramids by more enterprising vendors or divided by color upon handwoven cloths."

The other chile of choice in the Andes is the red or yellow, apple-shaped rocoto of the *pubescens* species. It is grown today in the Andes from Bolivia to Colombia, mostly in small family plots. It is also cultivated in the highland areas of Central America and Mexico. The rocotos are renowned for their pungency, and there is a Peruvian expression about them, "llevanta muertos," meaning they are hot enough to raise the dead. According to chile expert Dr. Jean Andrews, in the town of Huanta, Peru, rocotos are described as *gringo huanuchi,* "will kill a gringo." They are highly aromatic and flavorful in addition to their heat. The ripe pods are used fresh because their thick flesh makes them difficult to dry. They are often stuffed with cheese or sausage and baked.

Rocotos are the only chiles with black seeds, and *pubescens* is the only domesticated species that has no wild form; however, two wild species, *C. cardenasii* and *C. eximium,* are closely related. The center of origin for this species is Bolivia, and according to botanist Charles Heiser, it was probably domesticated around 6,000 B.C., making it one of the oldest domesticated plants in the Americas. Heiser went on to cite Garcilaso de la Vega (1609), that *pubescens* was "the most common pepper among the Incas, just as it is today in Cuzco, the former capital of the Incan empire."

It was in the Andes that the great Incan civilization came to depend upon the ajís and rocotos as their principal spice and a major crop. Farming determined nearly every aspect of Incan society: the calendar, religion, law, and even war. It has been estimated that more varieties of foods and medicinal plants were systematically cultivated in the Andes than anywhere else in the world at any time. The result of the Incan agricultural expertise included 240 varieties of potatoes, nearly as many kinds of beans, twenty types of maize, plus sweet potatoes, peanuts, pineapples, chocolate, avocados, papayas, tomatoes, and—of course—many types of the beloved chile pepper.

The Incan historian Garcilaso de la Vega, known as *El Inca,* wrote in detail about chile peppers and their place in Incan culture. In his *Royal Commentaries of the Incas* (1609), he noted that chiles were the favorite fruit of the Indians, who ate them with everything they cooked, "whether stewed, boiled, or roasted."

One reason for the popularity of pods was that the Incas worshipped the chile pepper as one of the four brothers of their creation myth.

"Agar-Uchu," or "Brother Chile Pepper," was believed to be the brother of the first Incan king. Garcilaso de la Vega observed that the chile pods were perceived to symbolize the teachings of the early Incan brothers. Chile peppers were thus regarded as holy plants, and the Incas' most rigorous fasts were those prohibiting all chiles. The Aymaras, an Andean tribe conquered by the Incas in the fifteenth century, had a saying that went: "Am I your salt or chile that you always have me in your mouth and speak ill of me?"

According to *El Inca*, the Incas raised three or four varieties of chiles. The first was called *rócot uchu*, "thick pepper," which described the long, thick pods that matured to yellow, red, and purple. Despite the adjective "rócot," the most likely identification of these chiles would be the ají species, *Capsicum baccatum*. Garcilaso forgot the name of the next type but wrote that it was used exclusively by the royal household. The third chile he described was *chinchi uchu*, which "resembles exactly a cherry with its stalk." This type, with its name and cherry-like pods both still intact, has survived to this day in Peru and Bolivia; it is the rocoto. *El Inca* noted that the *chinchi uchu* was "incomparably stronger than the rest and only small quantities of it are found, wherefore it is most esteemed."

The varieties of ajís were used extensively with Andean foodstuffs such as maize, potatoes, and quinoa, three of the most common vegetable crops grown by the Inca. According to the historian Bernabe Cobo, "of whole maize with some greens and chile they make a dish called *motepatasca*, cooking the maize until it burst." Maize was extremely important to the Inca, and it was primarily used to make breads and *chicha*, a beer that was their favorite intoxicant. *Locro*, a thick stew, was made with corn kernels, potatoes, ajís, meat, and beans.

Quinoa was also extensively cultivated, and it was so vital to the Inca that it was considered to be sacred. In Quecha, the language of the Incas, it was referred to as the "mother grain." It was also combined with ajís and potatoes in stews. We have used quinoa and ajís in recipes such as Ensalada con Quinoa de Peru (Peruvian Quinoa Salad, p. 228) and Ensalada con Quinoa de Bolivia (Bolivian Quinoa Salad, p. 230).

It is interesting to note that although the Inca cultivated a large number of varieties of potatoes, there was little legend and lore associated with them. "Despite the fact that the Inca were of highland origin themselves," wrote food historian Sophie Coe, "they consistently exalted maize and ignored what must have been their ancestral staple, the potato." Coe also noted, "Travelers visiting Peruvian markets today see a range of potato varieties undreamed of in their homeland. The tastes and textures vary as much as the looks, and Peruvians consider our commercial potatoes watery, insipid, and boring."

The Inca developed the technique of freeze-drying potatoes by setting them out at night to freeze and then squeezing the water out of them and allowing them to dry. The result was called *chuño,* and the preserved potatoes were usually added to soups or stews. Some of the best potato and ají recipes have survived to this day and are included in Chapter 8, including Llapingachos (Ecuadorian Spiced Potato Cakes, p. 222), and Papas Arequipeña (Potatoes in Peanut and Cheese Sauce, p. 223).

Most of the common folk ate the grains and potatoes, while the meats were generally reserved for the Inca nobility. Some of the meat and ají dishes were rather unusual, such as raw liver or llama entrails chopped up with fresh rocoto pods, as well as the infamous Andean rodent, the guinea pig or *cuy.* According to Bernabe Cobo, "The Indians eat this little animal with the skin on, only removing the hair as if it were a suckling pig. For them it is a great delicacy, and they cook it whole, gutted, with much chile and smooth pebbles from the river." The pebbles were heated in a fire and were used to cook the guinea pig. The *cuy* today provides more than fifty percent of the animal protein eaten in Peru!

Chile Pepper's David Parrish, who explored the foods of Ecuador, noted: "In most towns you can find some food stand that serves this rodent; it's usually just grilled whole over a fire until the meat is tender and the skin is crispy. Of course, being the intrepid eater that I am, I tried some. It was nothing extraordinary, and like most light meats of uncommon origin, it tasted somewhat like chicken. But, a little *cuy,* a little salsa, a cold beer (well, warm beer), and I had no complaints."

Other meats combined with ajís included the American camelids, the wild guanaco and vicuña, and the domesticated alpaca and llamas. Llamas were reserved exclusively for the Inca royalty, and none of the commoners were allowed to kill or eat any of them. The hearts of the camelids were particularly prized, and the Inca probably invented the dish that lives on today, *anticuchos,* chunks of heart (beef is used now) that have been marinated in a spicy vinegar and are then grilled and basted with ají-spiced oil. Our recipes for *anticuchos* are found in Chapter 3.

Today, the pervasiveness of chiles in the Andes lives on. The hottest city in the region is Arequipa, at the foot of the Misti Volcano in southern Peru.

The dishes from that city are so hot that restaurants in Lima list menu items as "arequipeño," meaning that diners should use caution when eating them.

Mary Dempsey, who wrote about Peru for *Chile Pepper* magazine, observed: "Peruvians will argue about Arequipa residents' claims that they are the nation's thinkers or have the country's most beautiful main plaza, but there is no dispute that the hearty food from this region is consistently delicious and mercilessly hot. The reputation comes from the unchecked use of rocotos, which have a fire engine red color that is not only decorative, but illustrative as a danger signal. Unsuspecting tourists in Arequipa frequently provide free restaurant entertainment for the locals who watch with great interest when novices bite into the raw pieces of rocotos garnishing their plates. Even die-hard chileheads admit this pepper is a killer, and Peruvians themselves claim that if anything can raise the dead, it is a rocoto." Two perfect examples of Arequipa heat are Salsa de Arequipa (Potato Sauce Arequipa-Style, p. 20), and Papas a la Huancaina (Potatoes Huancayo-Style, pp. 224–226), another dish with an ají-spiced cheese sauce.

Malaguetas and More: The Amazon

After the Andean region, chiles are most prevalent in Brazilian cookery and occur in many dishes. In Brazil and the Amazon basin, there are two main species we are concerned with, *C. chinense* and *frutescens,* the habanero and tabasco relatives, respectively. The malagueta pepper grows wild in the Amazon basin in Brazil, where the species probably originated. It is cultivated in scattered small plots, according to some sources. No domesticated *frutescens* has ever been found in an archaeological site in Middle or South America, but ethnobotanists speculate the domestication site was probably Panama, and from there it spread to Mexico and the Caribbean. The pods are borne erect and measure from ½- to 1½-inches long and ¼- to ⅜-inch wide. Immature pods are yellow or green, maturing to bright red.

An interesting botanical mystery crops up with the malagueta pepper from Brazil because it has virtually the same name as the melegueta pepper from West Africa. The mystery arises from the fact that the two peppers are completely unrelated botanically and in appearance. The African melegueta (*Aframomum melegueta*) is a reed-like plant with red berries, while the Brazilian malagueta is very similar to the tabasco chile that is the basis of the famous sauce.

The melegueta pepper enjoyed great popularity during the Elizabethan Age in England, primarily through trade with Portugal. Some food historians consider that since the word "melegueta" was already a Portuguese term for spicy berry, this name was transferred to a Brazilian red chile pepper of even more pungency, sometime after the Portuguese settlement of Brazil. This scenario follows a pattern that Christopher Columbus began when he misnamed chiles as pepper. The malagueta chile peppers, it seems, were given the closest common name when they were "discovered" by Europeans. Interestingly enough, the African meleguetas were eventually imported into Surinam and Guyana, where they were grown commercially.

But we are using the *Capsicum* version of the malagueta in this book. The most common use for the pods is making hot sauces; the malaguetas are crushed, salted, fermented, and combined with vinegar. A typical Brazilian sauce recipe is Môlho Malagueta (p. 22); another is Môlho de Pimenta com Limão (p. 23), which combines malagueta chiles with limes. The malagueta pods can also be used fresh in salsas and can be dried for adding to stir-fry dishes.

As far as the habanero relatives are concerned, the Amazon basin was the center of origin for the *chinense* species, famous for having the hottest chiles of them all. The oldest known *chinense* ever found was the 6,500 year-old intact pod found in Guitarrero Cave in Peru.

Bernabé Cobo, a naturalist who traveled throughout South America during the early seventeenth century, was probably the first European to study the *chinense* species. He estimated that there were at least forty different varieties of chiles, "some as large as limes or large plums; others, as small as pine nuts or even grains of wheat, and between the two extremes are many different sizes. No less variety is found in color . . . and the same difference is found in form and shape."

Chinense is the most important cultivated pepper east of the Andes in South America. There is a great diversity of pod shape (from chiltepin-sized berries to elongated pods) and heat levels ranging from zero to the hottest ever measured. They are green at immaturity and mature to red, orange, yellow, purple, or white. The wild *chinense* varieties have numerous local names in Spanish, Portuguese, and Indian dialects that translate as "fish eye," "parakeet's eye," and "blowgun pepper." At some point in time, Native Americans transferred the *chinense* from the Amazon Basin into the Caribbean, where land races developed on nearly every island.

The popularity of chiles in Brazilian cookery is the result of three factors: the prevalence of chiles in the Amazon Basin, their combination with foods introduced by the Portuguese, and the fact that the first African slaves readily adopted the native chiles. Brazilian cuisine was influenced more by African sources than its own native Indian tribes because, in colonial times, the Portuguese colonials totally depended upon African cooks who utilized both Brazilian and imported West African foodstuffs. There is even a saying in Brazil today, *A mais preta a cozinheira, o melhor a comida,* the blacker the cook, the better the food.

According to Tita Libín, who researched the subject for *Chile Pepper* magazine, chiles and religion collide in Bahia. "Bahia is where the African religions blended with Catholicism," she wrote, "creating a very unique synthesis, transforming their magical gods into the form of Catholic saints. It was necessary for the African slaves to make this transformation because their religion was deemed unacceptable to the authorities of the day. The slaves pretended to adopt Catholicism, but instead incorporated the Saints into their own religion, hiding the statues for rituals such as Magic Candomble ceremonies which only the 'initiated' were allowed to witness."

Tita went on to describe the the ceremonies. "Nowadays outsiders and tourists are sometimes permitted as spectators at these 'voodoo' ceremonies, but very few understand the sequence of the ritual. The followers who congregate to receive a particular Orixa or Saint are always dressed in white. At certain times in the ceremony, a specific Orixa possesses the body of one of the initiated for a few moments, promising the rest of the followers of the sect better times ahead. After the sacred ordeal is over, the people partake in a feast prepared with the favorite foods of the participating Saint."

In addition to a favorite food, each Orixa has a specific Catholic Saint counterpart, greeting, color of dress, day, and element. A recurring ingredient in most of the Orixa recipes is the malagueta chile. Examples of these "voodoo" foods are Arroz de Huaca (Oxala's Rice, p. 212), Bobó de Camarão (Bahian Spicy Shrimp, p. 188), and Vatapá com Frutos do Mar (p. 76), a dish that combines shrimp, malagueta chiles, coconut, peanuts, and tomatoes. In the coastal city of Salvador de Bahia, the dish is very spicy, with either dried or fresh chiles added. In more tourist-influenced areas such as Rio de Janiero, *vatapá* is generally not so spicy.

Aside from the Andes and the Amazon basin, food from the rest of South America is not so uniformly spicy. Rather, certain fiery dishes will leap out from among its blander counterparts, and we have included such recipes from most of the other countries on the continent.

Now, because it is shaped somewhat like a chile pod, we might expect Argentina to have some heat. But *Chile Pepper* writer Susan Hazen-Hammond found only a few fiery dishes when she explored that country, looking for chiles. In her story about the famed "ají p-p," the bad word chile, she wrote that people in Argentina usually prefer to talk about that chile rather than eat it.

"Still," she wrote, "even though they didn't eat hot in those days, they loved to talk hot. As a boy, Eduardo [Fuss, Hazen-Hammond's husband] often heard adults laughing about the fabled Putapario, a pepper so hot that it produced in the eater an unstoppable urge to shout the most vulgar oath any Argentine could imagine: 'What prostitute gave birth to you?'

"Back then, in the late 1940s, it seemed that this was all they knew about these explosive ajíes, as Argentines call chile peppers of any species." Susan collected seeds from a number of varieties of chiles she found in Argentina, and most of them turned out to be *Capsicum baccatum,* the familiar ají.

The Spicy Legacy of the Maya

Central America also has its pockets of heat. As is true of South America, the cuisines of some countries have embraced chile peppers with more fervor than others. Panama and Costa Rica, for example, have some spicy dishes but the overall cuisine is not as spicy as those of Belize or Guatemala. Guatemala has a fiery cuisine second only to Mexico in terms of chile usage—perhaps because of its Mayan heritage.

When the Europeans arrived in the New World, people of Mayan ancestry lived in southern Mexico, the Yucatán Peninsula, Belize, Guatemala, and parts of Honduras and El Salvador. The Mayan civilization had long passed its height by that time, so there are no Spanish observations about their classic culture. All that exist today are European observations of their descendants; Mayan hieroglyphics, which are slowly being transliterated; and ethnological observations of the present Maya Indians, whose food habits have changed little in twenty centuries.

By the time the Mayas reached the peak of their civilization in southern Mexico and the Yucatán Peninsula, around A.D. 500, they had a highly developed system of agriculture. Maize was their most important crop, followed closely by beans, squash, chiles, and cacao. Perhaps as many as thirty different varieties of chiles were cultivated, and they were sometimes planted in plots by themselves, but more often in fields already containing tomatoes and sweet potatoes. There were three species of chiles grown by the Maya and their descendants in Central America: *annuum, chinense,* and *frutescens*— and they were all imports from other regions. The *annuums* probably originated in Mexico, while the *frutescens* came from Panama, and the *chinense* from the Amazon Basin via the Caribbean. The Mayas also cultivated cotton, papayas, vanilla beans, cacao, manioc, and agave.

The importance of chiles is immediately seen in the most basic Mayan foods. According to food historian Sophie Coe, "The beans . . . could be cooked in plain water or water in which toasted or untoasted chiles had been steeped. Such a chile 'stock' might be called the basis of the cuisine, so frequently does it turn up. It is everything from the tortilla accompaniment of the very poorest peasant to the liquid for cooking the turkey for the greatest celebrations. There is even a reference to it in the *Popul Vuh* where the grandmother grinds chiles and mixes them with broth, and the broth acts as a mirror in which the rat on the rafters is reflected for the hero twins to see."

For breakfast the Maya ate a gruel of ground maize spiced with chile peppers, which is usually called *atole* but is sometimes known as *pozol.* A modern equivalent would be cornmeal or *masa* mixed with water and ground red chiles to make the consistency of a milkshake. A favorite drink was chocolate mixed with water, honey, and chile powder.

For the main, or evening meal, stews of vegetables and meats heavily spiced with chiles were served. One of these was *chacmole,* which combined venison with chile, achiote, allspice, and tomato—it was an offering to the gods as well as a nourishing entree. Various reports describe sauces made with chiles and black beans being wrapped in corn tortillas, which may be the earliest references to enchiladas. Enchilada sauces were made with chiles, toasted squash and pumpkin seeds, epazote, and Mexican oregano. Black beans were also served enchilada-style in tortillas with chile sauces. As Sophie Coe notes, "The accepted wisdom was that tortillas and beans were boring; it took chile to make the saliva flow."

The Maya seem to have invented tamales too, as the Spanish chronicler Gonzalo Fernández de Oviedo reported in 1526, "They brought certain well made baskets, one with the *pasticci* [filled pies] of maize dough stuffed with chopped meat. . . . They ate it all, and praised that dish *pasticci,* which tasted as if it were spiced. It was reddish inside, with a good quantity of that pepper of the Indies which is called *asci* [the Antillean word for chile, modernized to ají]." Mayan tamales were quite sophisticated, with many different fillings, including toasted squash seeds, deer hearts, quail, egg yolks, dove breasts, squash blossoms, and black beans.

The Maya kept domesticated turkeys, ducks, bees, and dogs, and their main game animals were deer, birds, iguana, and wild boar. Armadillos and manatees were considered delicacies. As with the Inca, meat dishes were reserved for Mayan royalty. Jocon (Chicken in Green Sauce with Smoked Chiles, p. 154) is a good example of a Mayan poultry dish that has resisted European influences; the only non-New World ingredients are garlic, onions, and chicken. The Mayas, of course, would have substituted duck or turkey for the chicken, and any of these fowls are acceptable in Jocon and also in Guisado Maya de Pavo (Mayan Turkey Stew, p. 167), which is a predecessor of the green chile stew served today in New Mexico. Pollo en Salsa de Pipián Rojo (Chicken in Red Pipian Sauce, p. 152) also has the Mayan influence of squash seeds, which are combined with chiles for a uniquely flavored sauce.

Chiles are highly visible today in areas with a Mayan heritage. In the Yucatán Peninsula, descendants of the Maya still grow habaneros, tomatoes, and onions in boxes or hollowed-out tree trunks that are raised up on four posts for protection against pigs and hens. These container gardens are usually in the yard of the house, near the kitchen. The most popular chile in Guatemala is the *chile de cobán*, a variety of piquin with round to slightly elongated pods that are smoke-dried over wood and have a powerful, smoky taste. Our recipe for Jocon features these chiles, or if they are unavailable, use the similarly smoky chipotles.

Central America is becoming quite a chile pepper growing mecca. The McIlhenny Company of Avery Island, Louisiana, grows the majority of tabascos for its famous sauce in Mexico, Honduras, and Colombia. Costa Rica is the source of habaneros and other chiles for hot sauces, and we have heard about substantial growing operations in Panama and Guatemala. We have visited growing and processing operations in Belize and Costa Rica, and believe us, it's a real thrill to see five-foot tall plants loaded with habaneros—in fact, almost as much of a thrill as cooking and eating the hot and spicy Latin dishes that follow.

2

Los Ajís Latinos
Spiced-Up Salsas

Versatile and varied, the chile-filled *salsas* of Latin America are sauces that are fresh or cooked, and thick or thin. They range from incendiary liquified habaneros to ají pastes, and their principal use is to concentrate fresh chiles into a form with a longer shelf life. Our first recipe is just such a chile paste, Ají Molido (p. 14). It is our standard substitute for fresh chiles in any recipe in this book. The heat will vary depending on the chiles you use, but remember—most concentrates of chiles are rather hot. Another basic South American sauce is Aceite de Achiote (Achiote Oil, p. 15), which can be used as a brightly colored substitute for vegetable oil.

In the Andes, ají salsas are used to add heat to bland foods such as potatoes, beans, corn, and manioc. Salsa de Ají (Ecuadorian Hot Salsa, p. 16), is similar to the Mexican *pico de gallo*, but the chiles are applied with a twist: they are pureed before being added. Salsa Picante de Peru (Peruvian Hot Salsa, p. 17), and Pebre (Chilean Hot Salsa, p. 18), also resemble the Mexican favorite, varying only in the herbs used to flavor them. Another versatile ají sauce is Salsa Peruana Ají de Miguel (Miguel's Peruvian Ají Sauce, p. 19). Two truly different sauces from Peru and Ecuador for flavoring potatoes are Salsa de Arequipa (p. 20), which combines ajís with walnuts, cheese, and shrimp to flavor potatoes and fried fish, and Salsa de Mani (Hot and Spicy Peanut Sauce, p. 21), which features peanuts and cheese—along with ajís, of course.

The Brazilian sauces are next. Môlho Malagueta (p. 22) features that fiery tabasco relative, the malagueta, in a vinegar-oil solution. Môlho de Pimenta com Limão (Hot Pepper Sauce with Lime, p. 23) has the same chile steeped in garlic and lemon juice. Both are great with seafood and stews, while Môlho de Acarajé (Chile-Shrimp Sauce, p. 24), is served over fritters or potatoes. Farofa de Malagueta (Brazilian Chile Condiment, p. 25) is made with manioc flour and is served over entrees.

The Latin American Caribbean is represented by two recipes. Salsa de Habanero (p. 26) is quite similar to commercial Belizean hot sauces sold in the United States and Canada. Pickapeppa Hot Sauce (p. 27), no relation to the commercial Jamaican sauce of the same name, is a sweet and tasty sauce from Guyana.

Argentina, which isn't traditionally spicy, makes an appearance with three sauces to add heat at the table. Salsa Satánica (Satan's Seafood Sauce, p. 28), is a popular restaurant sauce from Buenos Aires. Chimichurri (Hot Vinegar-Parsley Sauce, p. 29) is served with charbroiled meats and poultry. And Mama's Chimichurri (p. 30), collected by our friend Susan Hazen-Hammond, is a version designed for beefsteak.

Our final three sauces are barbecue sauces from Brazil, Argentina, and Venezuela. Môlho de Churrasco (Brazilian Barbecue Sauce, p. 31) features herbs, malaguetas, and plenty of vinegar; Salsa Criolla (Creole Barbecue Sauce, p. 32), from Argentina, is onion and mustard-based. Guasacaca (p. 33), from Venezuela, is a fitting conclusion because it is our most unusual barbecue sauce, with avocados and habaneros.

Ají Molido

(Chile Paste)

This South American paste can be used as a substitute whenever fresh chiles are called for. It will keep for two weeks or more in the refrigerator. For longer storage, increase the vinegar and reduce the amount of olive oil.

20 fresh yellow ají chiles, seeds and stems removed, chopped, or substitute yellow wax hot chiles or jalapeños

¼ cup olive oil

1 clove garlic, minced

2 tablespoons vinegar

1 teaspoon salt

Combine all ingredients in a food processor and puree to a fine paste.

Variations: For a red paste, substitute 15 dried New Mexican red chiles, soaked in water. For a green paste, substitute 10 New Mexican green chiles. For a much hotter paste, add 5 habanero chiles. All chiles should have the seeds and stems removed.

Yield: About 1 cup

Heat Scale: Hot

Aceite de Achiote
(Achiote Oil)

This oil is used both to color and to flavor dishes. Use it in place of vegetable oil in the recipes in this book. Look for annatto (achiote) seeds that are a bright-reddish color; seeds that are brownish in color are old and have probably lost much of their flavor.

1   cup best quality olive oil or high quality vegetable oil

½   cup annatto (achiote) seeds, crushed

1   dried malagueta chile, or substitute piquin or Japanese

1   bay leaf (optional)

Combine all ingredients in a non-reactive heavy saucepan and allow the mixture to steep for 40 minutes, stirring occasionally.

Then, on the stove, bring the mixture to a low and gentle boil while stirring continuously. Remove the saucepan from the heat and allow the mixture to cool thoroughly.

Strain the oil through a very fine sieve and then pour the strained oil into a bottle and cap tightly. This oil will remain usable up to 6 months if it is refrigerated and capped tightly.

Yield: 1 cup

Heat Scale: Medium

Salsa de Ají
(Ecuadorian Hot Salsa)

This is a classic Latin American salsa recipe collected in Ecuador by David Parrish, who wrote about his travels there in *Chile Pepper* magazine. Although this recipe calls for the use of an electric blender, one can follow the traditional method of using a mortar and pestle.

2 large tomatoes, seeds removed, finely chopped
1 medium onion, finely chopped
1 tablespoon chopped fresh cilantro

4 large ají chiles, seeds and stems removed, chopped, or substitute yellow wax hot chiles or jalapeños
½ cup water
Salt to taste

Combine the tomatoes, onion, and cilantro in a bowl. Place the chiles, water, and 3 tablespoons of the tomato, onion, cilantro mixture in a blender or processor and puree until smooth. Add the chile puree to the remaining tomato mixture and mix well.

Salt to taste.

Variations: Ecuadorians are very fond of adding beans to their salsa. The most popular beans are the *lupini,* which are large white beans about the size of lima beans. Just add the cooked beans directly to the salsa. Or, add 1 teaspoon peanut butter with the chiles in the blender and follow the above recipe.

Yield: 1 to 2 cups
Heat Scale: Medium

Salsa Picante de Peru

(Peruvian Hot Salsa)

This recipe is from Mary Dempsey and was published in *Chile Pepper* magazine. It is traditionally served with Anticuchos Picantes (p. 62) and corn on the cob, but it's a great accompaniment for any grilled meat.

3	fresh ají chiles, seeds and stems removed, minced, or substitute red serranos or jalapeños	4	cloves garlic, peeled and crushed
½	medium onion, minced	2	tablespoons vegetable oil
2	green onions, minced including the greens	2	tablespoons wine vinegar

Combine all ingredients in a bowl and let sit for at least an hour to blend the flavors.

Yield: ¾ cup

Heat Scale: Hot

Next They'll Ban Thumbsucking in Restaurants

"There are only three restrictions on hot pepper use in Peru. They are not eaten by small children, nursing mothers, or the sick. It is common to hear doctors putting patients *en dieta,* which is nothing more than a temporary ban on ají and rocoto consumption. As a punitive measure, thumbsucking toddlers may have the offending finger dipped in ají juice, but more than one Peruvian, laughing, will theorize that this only serves to start the ají addiction." —Mary Dempsey

Pebre

(Chilean Hot Salsa)

Here is the classic hot sauce of Chile, one that is served with grilled or roasted meats. The type of chiles used varies considerably, depending on availability and the cook's preference.

2 tablespoons olive oil	2 cloves garlic, minced
1 tablespoon red wine vinegar	½ cup minced onion
⅓ cup water	½ cup minced cilantro
4 fresh ají chiles, seeds and stems removed, minced, or substitute 1 jalapeño or 1 habanero	1 teaspoon minced fresh oregano Salt to taste

Combine the olive oil, vinegar, and water in a bowl and beat with a whisk. Add the remaining ingredients, mix well, and let stand for 2 hours to blend the flavors.

Yield: 1½ cups

Heat Scale: Hot

Salsa Peruana Ají de Miguel

(Miguel's Peruvian Ají Sauce)

We grow a lot of Peruvian ají chiles in our garden every year, and we always put aside a large bag of them to take to Miguel, our computer wizard friend from Peru. On Mary Jane's second or third trip to Miguel's (it was a bumper harvest of chiles), he was having a late lunch with this ají sauce over his rice.

½ cup olive oil	¼ teaspoon salt
4 or more fresh ají chiles, seeds and stems removed, minced, or substitute yellow wax hot chiles or jalapeños	¼ teaspoon freshly ground black pepper
2 cloves garlic, minced	1 tablespoon fresh lime juice

Heat the oil in a small skillet, and when it's hot, add the chiles and the garlic, lower the heat, and stir constantly to avoid burning the garlic. Add the remaining ingredients and stir. Simmer for ten minutes and then serve warm over rice or pasta.

Yield: ¾ cup

Heat Scale: Hot

Salsa de Arequipa

(Potato Sauce Arequipa-Style)

From Arequipa, Peru, one of the hottest (chile-wise) cities in Latin America, comes this unusual, delicious sauce that is traditionally served over boiled and sliced potatoes that are garnished with lettuce, olives, and hard-boiled egg slices. Try it over fried fish as well.

8   dried yellow ají chiles, seeds and stems removed, soaked in water to soften and pureed, or substitute 6 New Mexican red chiles

3   saltine-type crackers, crushed

¼   cup walnuts, ground in a spice mill

½   cup grated Montery Jack cheese

¼   cup vegetable oil

¼   cup chopped onion

1   clove garlic, mashed

2   hard-boiled eggs, minced

12 cooked shrimp, peeled and mashed

Milk

Salt and freshly ground black pepper to taste

In a large bowl, combine the chiles, crackers, walnuts, cheese, vegetable oil, onion, garlic, eggs, and shrimp and mix well to make a thick paste. Drizzle in the milk as needed and, using a potato masher, transform the paste into a thick sauce. Add salt and pepper to taste.

Yield: About 2½ cups

Heat Scale: Medium

Salsa de Mani
(Hot and Spicy Peanut Sauce)

Our Ecuadorian food source, Winifred Galarza, said this is a commonly made sauce served over potatoes in Ecuador. The amount of chile in the recipe can be adjusted to be mild or wild, however you wish. This side dish would also add spice to any meat or seafood dish for a truly exotic dinner.

½ cup peanuts
¼ cup cream
¼ cup milk
⅓ cup peanut oil
¼ teaspoon salt
¼ teaspoon freshly ground black pepper

1½ teaspoons ají chile powder, or substitute piquin or cayenne
1 small onion, peeled and quartered
½ cup grated Muenster or crumbled feta cheese

Place all of the ingredients in a blender or food processor and blend at high speed for a few seconds, or until smooth. Place in a pan and heat over low heat for 5 minutes, stirring constantly. Do not boil the sauce. Serve over hot cooked potatoes.

Yield: 2 cups

Heat Scale: Mild

Môlho Malagueta

(Malagueta Sauce)

Here is a basic Brazilian hot sauce featuring the malaguetas. It is simple, powerful, and can be added to any recipe in this book (except desserts) to spice it up.

1   cup fresh or dried malagueta chiles, or substitute tabascos or piquins, stems removed, left whole

1   wine bottle (750 ml.), washed in boiling water and dried, with cork

1   cup vinegar
     Olive oil to fill bottle

Place the chiles in the wine bottle, add the vinegar and olive oil, and cork the bottle securely. Place the bottle in the refrigerator and let the chiles steep for at least 2 weeks, shaking the bottle whenever you think about it.

Yield: 750 milliliters

Heat Scale: Hot

Môlho de Pimenta com Limão
(Hot Pepper Sauce with Lime)

This hot sauce from Pernambuco is commonly served in a small bowl at Brazilian meals to spice up such dishes as *feijoada* and seafood stews. It features the malagueta pepper, that close relative of the tabasco pepper.

6   fresh malagueta chiles, or substitute piquins, seeds and stems removed, minced
1   clove garlic, minced
1   medium onion, minced
½   teaspoon salt
½   cup lemon or lime juice

Combine all ingredients and allow to sit at room temperature for 2 hours to blend all the flavors.

Variation: Make a paste by pureeing the peppers, garlic, onion, and salt in a blender. Add the lemon or lime juice and stir well.

Yield: ¾ *cup*

Heat Scale: Hot

Spicy Royalty

"The food of the Bahians is flavored with the blood and the tears from the slaves in a land where *pimenta malagueta* is queen and black pepper is king and cinnamon are princes. Black pepper is still called *pimenta de reino,* which literally means 'pepper of the crown,' and is grown and widely used in most of the Brazilian dishes." —Tita Libín

Môlho de Acarajé
(Chile-Shrimp Sauce)

This Brazilian sauce is traditionally served over black-eyed pea fritters (*acarajé*, called accra in the West Indies) but can also be spread over other bland foods such as potatoes. It has an intense shrimp flavor and high heat. It is traditionally made with *dende* (palm oil) but we have substituted one with less saturated fat.

6   large shrimp, cooked, shelled, deveined, and mashed

1   onion, minced

5   fresh malagueta chiles, seeds and stems removed, minced, or substitute tabascos, Thais, or piquins

½   teaspoon salt

3   tablespoons corn oil, or more if needed

With a mortar and pestle, crush together the shrimp, onion, chiles, and salt to make a paste.

Heat the oil and sauté the paste for 10 minutes, stirring constantly.

Variation: Add 1 teaspoon minced cilantro and ½ teaspoon ground ginger to the paste.

Yield: About ¾ cup

Heat Scale: Hot

Farofa de Malagueta

(Brazilian Chile Condiment)

Farofas are Brazilian condiments made with manioc flour, which is available at Latin markets. They are commonly sprinkled over the top of Brazilian meals such as Bifes (p. 134). *Farofieros,* cooks who specialize in the preparation of *farofas,* have been known to make eighty or more variations.

¼   cup palm oil, or substitute vegetable oil with 3 teaspoons paprika added

1   cup chopped onion

2   hard-boiled eggs, chopped

1   teaspoon minced fresh or pickled malagueta chile, or substitute piquin (dry chiles can be used if soaked in water first)

2   cups manioc flour or dried bread crumbs

Heat the palm oil in a frying pan and fry the onions until golden brown. Add the hard-boiled eggs and sauté the mixture for 1 minute. Next add the chiles and manioc flour stirring constantly until the mixture turns golden.

Yield: 3 cups

Heat Scale: Medium

Salsa de Habanero

(Belizean Habanero Sauce)

To preserve the distinctive flavor of the habaneros, don't cook them with the sauce, but add them afterwards. This sauce will keep for weeks in the refrigerator. Use it to spice up eggs, sandwiches, soups, and seafood.

1	small onion, chopped	10	fresh habanero chiles, seeds
1	tablespoon vegetable oil		and stems removed, minced
½	cup chopped carrots	¼	cup lime juice
1	cup water		

Sauté the onion in the oil until soft. Add the carrots and water. Bring to a boil, reduce the heat, and simmer until the carrots are soft. Allow the mixture to cool at room temperature.

Add the habaneros and lime juice to the carrot mixture. Place the mixture in a blender and puree until smooth.

Yield: 1 cup

Heat Scale: Extremely Hot

Pickapeppa Hot Sauce

This is not the commercial sauce from Jamaica but rather a specialty from Georgetown, Guyana. It is served over seafood or used to spice up gravies and salad dressings.

12 dried "bird peppers" (chilte-pins), seeds and stems removed, crushed, or substitute piquins or Thai chiles

½ teaspoon dried mustard

3 tablespoons soy sauce

3 tablespoons lime juice

¼ cup ketchup

1 teaspoon salt

2 teaspoons brown sugar

1 cup dry sherry

Combine all ingredients in a bottle and refrigerate for at least a week to blend the flavors. Shake at least once a day.

Yield: 1½ cups

Heat Scale: Medium

Chile Conquers the Conquerers

Garcilaso de la Vega, *El Inca,* collected some chile anecdotes. Chiles were reputedly good for one's vision, were avoided by poisonous creatures, and were offered as gifts to appease Pizarro and his invading soldiers. As a culinary note, *El Inca* unconsciously predicted the spread of chile around the world when he noted, "All the Spaniards who come to Spain from the Indies are accustomed to it and prefer it to all Oriental spices." Thus the invaders were seduced by the fiery foods of the Incas!

Salsa Satánica

(Satan's Seafood Sauce)

Here's a surprisingly spicy sauce that is served in Buenos Aires restaurants and is also called fisherman's sauce. Serve it over any kind of seafood.

½ cup butter
½ cup ketchup
1   tablespoon Worcestershire sauce
1   tablespoon crushed onion
1   tablespoon tarragon vinegar

½ teaspoon garlic salt
2   teaspoons bottled hot sauce of choice or Salsa de Habanero (p. 26)
¼ cup brandy

Melt the butter in a saucepan. Add the ketchup, Worcestershire, onion, vinegar, garlic salt, and habanero sauce. Simmer for 5 minutes. Add the brandy and simmer 5 more minutes. Remove from the heat and cool.

Yield: About 1½ cups

Heat Scale: Medium

Chimichurri
(Hot Vinegar-Parsley Sauce)

There is a minor debate about whether or not this Argentinian sauce should contain chile peppers. As usual, there is no real answer because cooks tend to add them or not, according to taste. This sauce is served with broiled, roasted, or grilled meat and poultry.

¼ cup olive oil

1 cup red wine vinegar

2 tablespoons ají chile powder, or substitute New Mexican red chile powder

4 cloves garlic, minced

1 teaspoon crushed black peppercorns

1 teaspoon dried oregano

1 bay leaf, crushed

¼ cup minced parsley (or substitute Italian parsley)

Salt to taste

Combine the olive oil and vinegar in a bowl and beat with a whisk. Stir in the remaining ingredients, mix thoroughly, and allow to sit for 2 hours to blend the flavors.

Yield: 1½ cups

Heat Scale: Medium

Mama's Chimichurri

This version of *chimichurri* was collected by Susan Hazen-Hammond and is used more as a relish than a dipping sauce. As Susan suggested in her article in *Chile Pepper*, it is served at the table and spread over charbroiled steaks just before eating.

6 cloves garlic, minced

1 tablespoon chopped fresh parsley, or substitute dried

4 tablespoons lemon juice, fresh preferred

2 tablespoons olive oil

1 teaspoon crushed ají chiles, or substitute red chile such as New Mexican, piquin, or de Arbol

Salt and freshly ground black pepper to taste

Combine all the ingredients and place in a non-metallic jar. Allow the salsa to sit in the refrigerator overnight. Remove 1 hour before use and stir well. Just before serving, stir well again.

Note: This recipe requires advance preparation.

Yield: ¼ cup

Heat Scale: Mild

Môlho de Churrasco

(Brazilian Barbecue Sauce)

Brazilian barbecues are justly famous, and this sauce can be used for basting during the slow cooking process. Feel free to use it for American-style barbecues as well.

8	dried malagueta chiles, seeds and stems removed, crushed, or substitute piquin or Thai chiles	2	tablespoons minced Italian parsley
		1	teaspoon crushed rosemary
3	cups vinegar	2	teaspoons minced fresh basil leaves
1	teaspoon salt		
1	tablespoon sugar	2	teaspoons minced fresh thyme leaves
2	cloves garlic, crushed		
1	small onion, minced	2	teaspoons minced fresh marjoram or oregano leaves

Combine all ingredients in a glass jar, cover, and shake well. Let stand for at least 2 hours to blend the flavors. Store in a refrigerator until ready to use.

Yield: 4 cups

Heat Scale: Medium

Salsa Criolla

(Creole Barbecue Sauce)

There are many variations of this Creole sauce from Argentina, but this is our favorite. It is served with grilled, roasted, or barbecued meats, especially Matambre (pp. 127–128).

2   tablespoons ají chile powder, or substitute New Mexican red chile powder

2   teaspoons dry mustard

⅓   cup red wine vinegar

½   cup olive oil

2   cloves garlic, minced

2   onions, minced

3   ripe tomatoes, chopped fine

2   tablespoons minced Italian parsley

Salt to taste

Combine the chile powder and the mustard with a little vinegar to make a paste. Add the rest of the vinegar and the olive oil and beat with a whisk. Add the remaining ingredients, stir well, and allow to sit for 2 hours to blend the flavors.

Variation: Add 1 bell pepper and 1 jalapeño, both seeded and minced.

Yield: About 4 cups

Heat Scale: Medium

Guasacaca

(Barbecue Sauce from Venezuela)

This is by far the most unusual barbecue sauce in Latin America. Because it contains fresh avocados, it must be used immediately and cannot be stored. Use it to marinate and/or baste grilled or barbecued shrimp, beef slices, or chicken.

1 cup minced onion

2 cloves garlic, minced

1 habanero chile, seeds and stem removed, minced, or substitute 2 jalapeños

1 large ripe avocado, peeled and pit removed

2 cups peeled and chopped ripe tomatoes

1 cup olive oil

¼ cup red wine vinegar, or substitute lime juice

1 teaspoon prepared mustard

2 tablespoons minced parsley (Italian preferred)

Salt to taste

With a mortar and pestle, mash the onion, garlic, chile, avocado, and tomatoes into a paste (this may need to be done in batches). Add the remaining ingredients and blend well with a fork.

Yield: About 4 cups

Heat Scale: Medium

3

Aperitivos Picantes
Sharp Appetizers

antalizing and tasty, the appetizers of Latin America range from barely spicy to wickedly hot—depending, of course, on the chiles used in each tidbit. However, the first delight in this chapter, Salbutes (Spicy Tortilla Puffs, p. 37), from the Yucatán Peninsula, allows you to select your own heat scale with the judicious use of Belizean Habanero Sauce.

In much of Latin America, you'll find lush tropical forests and farms, which offer a wide variety of fruits and vegetables. That's why this chapter is loaded with them. Ensalada de Jicama y Naranja (Jicama and Orange Salad, p. 38) is a refreshing starter that relies on citrus, limes, and the apple-like flavor of jicama. And the avocado, a favorite ingredient in much of Latin America, takes top billing twice with the Brazilian hot dip, Verduras com Môlho Picante de Abacate (Vegetables with Spicy Avocado Sauce, p. 39), which acquires its heat from the malagueta chile, and Picante de Huevos (Egg and Avocado Appetizer, p. 40), which hails from Colombia. The onion, a marvelous vegetable that is often maligned (but still widely consumed), is featured in our Salgadinho com Queijo, Cebola, e Malaguetas (Onion Chile-Cheese Appetizer, p. 41). The sweetness of the onions, combined with the malagueta heat, sour cream, and Parmesan cheese, will be a hit at any party. Our Salgadinho de Camarão com Milho (Brazilian Corn and Shrimp Cupcakes, p. 42) are also Brazilian party favorites.

Seafood is a major staple in most Latin American countries, and our Frituras de Caracol Pastel (Colombian Conch Fritters, p. 43) are a good example of some of the varied and exotic choices available. Pastel Camarón y Ají con Espinaca (Shrimp and Ají Spinach Pie, p. 44) marries shellfish, chiles, nuts, cheese, and spinach for a healthy, spicy starter.

Carne, or meat, is still a special occasion meal in many areas of Latin America such as Ecuador, where the guinea pig provides the largest source of meat-based protein. Brazil and Argentina are exceptions to this, as they raise enormous herds of cattle on large ranches. Pork is also commonly used in appetizers; we offer Ensalada de Cerdo con Jalapeños (Nicaraguan Jalapeño Pork Salad, p. 46), and Albóndigas con Ajís, Uruguayan meatballs made with pork and ají chiles (p. 48). The Butifarra (Special Peruvian Sandwich, p. 49) calls for beef, which is slightly unusual for a dish from that country. And we've even included a bit of black magic in this cookbook, starting with the Bifes á la Criolla (Beef Creole, p. 50), a recipe from Brazil that is often served at voodoo ceremonies.

Maize, whether fresh off the cob, ground into meal, or boiled, baked, or stewed, offers an authentic basis to much Latin fiery fare. We have three appetizers that utilize this New World ingredient: Torrejas de Maíz Tierno (Fresh Corn Fritters, p. 51); Humitas Picantes (Spicy Corn Casserole, p. 52), and Humitas en Chala (Seasoned Pureed Tamales, p. 53). The latter gains its heat from ajís and its richness from an eclectic assortment of vegetables, cheese, and corn.

Do you have a good source for banana leaves? Well, if you do, you'll love the Nicaraguan Nacatamales (p. 54), which translates to small packages of incredible ingredients wrapped in banana leaves.

Other tasty appetizers you won't want to miss are empanadas. To make things interesting, we've included a base recipe, Empanadas de Nelly (p. 56), as well as exciting fillings including Relleno de Queso Picante (Spicy Cheese Filling, p. 58) from Argentina and Recheio de Camarão (Shrimp Stuffing, Bahian-Style, p. 59) from Brazil.

And finally, we would be remiss if we didn't include a few versions of *anticuchos,* one of Latin America's most famous appetizers. We've featured three different recipes. The first two are traditional and are made with beef hearts: Andean Anticuchos (Andean Shish Kebob with Hot Sauce, p. 60) and Anticuchos Picantes (Spicier Grilled Beef Heart, p. 62). A more modern version is our Argentinean Anticuchos (Skewered Spiced Sirloin, p. 64).

Salbutes

(Spicy Tortilla Puffs)

These fried, puffed-up tortillas are common throughout the Yucatán Peninsula. Although usually served as an appetizer, we enjoyed ours as a lunch entree sprinkled with liberal doses of an habanero hot sauce. This recipe is from *Chile Pepper* magazine food editor Nancy Gerlach.

2   cups masa harina
2   tablespoons flour
½   teaspoon baking powder
½   teaspoon salt
¾   cup water, or more if necessary
    Vegetable oil for frying
2   chicken breasts, poached, skin
    removed, shredded

1   small onion, chopped fine
2   tablespoons chopped cilantro
    Belizean Habanero Sauce (see
    recipe, p. 26), or your favorite
    bottled habanero sauce

Combine the masa, flour, baking powder, and salt. Add enough water to make a soft dough. Knead well and let the dough rest for 15 minutes.

Pinch off small amounts of the dough and roll into balls. With a rolling pin, roll the balls into small tortillas about 3 inches in diameter. Fry the tortillas on a hot griddle on both sides until the dough is dry but not brown.

Then fry the tortillas in hot oil for a minute or until both sides are brown and crisp. The tortillas should immediately puff up in the oil. Carefully remove and drain.

Top with the chicken, onions, cilantro, and sprinkle with Belizean Habanero Sauce (p. 26).

Yield: 4 to 6 servings

Heat Scale: Varies

Ensalada de Jicama y Naranja

(Jicama and Orange Salad)

Jicama is a Central American root crop with a refreshing texture and a taste reminiscent of apples. Here is Nancy Gerlach's version of a recipe from a Nicaraguan friend.

Juice of 2 limes
¼ teaspoon habanero chile powder, or substitute cayenne
2 small oranges, cut in segments

1 small jicama, julienne cut
3 green onions, thinly sliced
Chopped fresh cilantro

Combine the lime juice and habanero powder.

Arrange the orange segments on a platter and top with the jicama and onions. Pour the lime juice mixture over the salad, garnish with the cilantro, and serve.

Yield: 4 to 6 servings

Heat Scale: Medium

Verduras com Môlho Picante de Abacate

(Vegetables with Spicy Avocado Sauce)

Avocados are a luscious and sensuous treat; like jicama, they seem to bridge the gap between vegetables and fruits. In this Brazilian spicy sauce, avocados provide the essential flavor. The sauce can also be used as a salad dressing. Remember that the malagueta chiles are bright red when they are mature, so substitute fresh red piquins, tabascos, Thais, or even serranos.

1	tablespoon butter	1	tablespoon sugar
1½	teaspoons ketchup	3	drops Tabasco sauce
1	tablespoon warm water	2	fresh red malagueta chiles, chopped, or substitute piquins
1	tablespoon Worcestershire sauce	2	ripe avocados, peeled and pitted
1	tablespoon white vinegar		Sticks of celery, carrot, and jicama
¼	teaspoon salt		
½	teaspoon dry mustard		
5	whole cloves, crushed		

Combine all the ingredients except the vegetable sticks in a food processor and puree, adding more water if necessary. Chill for at least 30 minutes. Serve as a dip for the celery, carrots, and jicama.

Yield: 8 servings

Heat Scale: Medium

Picante de Huevos
(Egg and Avocado Appetizer)

Habaneros are grown in many Latin American countries, including Colombia, the origin of this recipe. Their fruity-hot flavor adds an excellent dimension to this specialty dish.

6	hard-boiled eggs, chopped	3	tablespoons finely chopped parsley
2	avocados, peeled, pitted, and chopped	2	tablespoons vinegar
1	fresh habanero, seeds and stem removed, finely chopped, or substitute 3 jalapeños	½	teaspoon salt
1	onion, finely chopped	3	mangoes, halved, seeds removed
			Fresh cilantro

Place all the ingredients except the mangoes and cilantro in a food processor or blender and blend at medium speed until very well combined and fairly smooth. Chill for several hours. Pour the sauce into the hollowed out section of the mango halves, and garnish with cilantro.

Yield: 4 to 6 servings

Heat Scale: Hot

Salgadinho com Queijo, Cebola, e Malaguetas

(Onion Chile-Cheese Appetizer)

This Brazilian appetizer is a light start before a full course meal. The red onions and Parmesan cheese add the right touch. The fruity drink, Brazilian Milk Punch (p. 245), would be an excellent accompaniment to this starter dish.

2 red onions, thinly sliced	½ teaspoon lime juice
2 fresh red malagueta chiles, seeds and stems removed, minced, or substitute piquins or serranos	12 puff pastry shells, commercially prepared
¾ cup sour cream	6 tablespoons freshly grated Parmesan cheese
	Salt and pepper to taste

Combine the onions with the chiles, sour cream, and lime juice, then cover and refrigerate. Bake the puff pastry shells according to the instructions on the box until ¾ done, then remove them from the oven. Let the pastry cool on the baking sheet, then evenly spread the onion mixture in each shell. Top the mixture in each pastry with the Parmesan cheese, salt, and pepper. Place the pastry lid on each shell and finish baking the shells until light brown. Serve immediately.

Yield: 12 servings

Heat Scale: Medium

Salgadinho de Camarão com Milho

(Brazilian Corn and Shrimp Cupcakes)

The cocktail hour is alive and well in Brazil and the rest of Latin America—although the said hour usually doesn't start until about 8 P.M.! These little appetizers are often served at cocktail parties accompanied by a spicy sauce such as Môlho de Pimenta com Limão (p. 23).

2	cups cooked corn kernels, drained	5	eggs, beaten
1	onion, minced	1½	cups cooked chopped shrimp
	Salt	1	tablespoon parsley, chopped
1	teaspoon malagueta chile powder, or substitute cayenne	1	tablespoon butter
		2	tablespoons cheddar cheese, grated
1	cup hot water	2	teaspoons cornstarch

Place the corn, onion, salt, and chile powder in a saucepan. Cover with the hot water, and bring to a boil. After 5 minutes, remove from the heat and drain well. Puree half the corn mixture in a blender until smooth, and combine with the unblended mixture. Place all the mixture in a bowl, and add the beaten eggs, shrimp, parsley, butter, cheese, and cornstarch. Mix well and check the seasoning. Add more salt if necessary.

Spray muffin tins with non-stick cooking oil, and fill ¾ full with batter. Set the muffin tins in a pan of water and bake in a 425°F oven for about 20 minutes, or until well browned and firm to the touch. Allow to cool slightly, then loosen the edges with a knife and turn out. Serve on platters along with a spicy sauce of your choice.

Yield: 18–20 muffins

Heat Scale: Medium

Frituras de Caracol

(Colombian Conch Fritters)

The conch shell is still used by fishermen as a blowing horn. However, the real magic is in the meat of the conch; these fritters highlight their wonderful taste. It is also said that the texture of the conch is similar to the most succulent steak. Serve the fritters with a hot sauce of choice from Chapter 2.

2 cups conch meat, pounded and finely chopped (clams make an acceptable substitute)

¼ cup grated onions

¼ cup finely chopped ripe olives

4 teaspoons finely chopped pimiento, or substitute cooked red bell pepper

1 teaspoon minced garlic

½ teaspoon basil

½ teaspoon tarragon

3 dashes bottled habanero hot sauce

1 habanero chile, seeds and stem removed, minced, or substitute 3 jalapeños

1 teaspoon sifted baking powder

½ cup sifted flour

1 egg, well beaten

Olive oil for frying

In a bowl, combine all of the ingredients except the baking powder, flour, egg, and olive oil and set aside. In another bowl, sift the baking powder and flour together and mix with the egg. Add the first mixture to the egg mixture, stir well, and let stand for 5 minutes. Place the oil in a frying pan and bring up to 380°F. Carefully drop dough balls into the oil and cook until brown. Remove with a slotted spoon and drain on paper towels.

Yield: About 20 fritters

Heat Scale: Hot

Pastel de Camarón y Ají con Espinaca

(Shrimp and Ají Spinach Pie)

This Peruvian dish is served in individual portions on fresh spinach leaves. To the Incas, the chile pepper was a holy plant, and that certainly makes sense since this combination of ajís, spinach, and cheese makes this a heavenly dish. The ajís or other chiles can be mashed in a mortar or a food processor to make a coarse paste.

2 cups frozen spinach, thawed, washed, and drained	Salt and freshly ground black pepper to taste
¼ cup chopped onions	3 eggs, beaten
1 clove garlic	½ cup grated cheddar cheese
Vegetable oil	1 dozen shrimp, parboiled, peeled, deveined
½ cup tomato juice	3 hard-boiled eggs, peeled and sliced
½ cup ground toasted peanuts	
¼ cup mashed fresh ají chiles, or substitute yellow wax hot chiles or New Mexican	

Place the spinach in a pan with sufficient water and cook gently for 5 minutes, stirring constantly to prevent from sticking to the bottom of the pan. Add more water if necessary. Remove from the heat and drain.

In another pan, sauté the onions and garlic in a little vegetable oil. Remove the garlic when it turns brown. Add the tomato juice, peanuts, chiles, salt and pepper and cook for 10 minutes.

Add the 3 beaten eggs to the spinach puree and mix well. Place half of the spinach puree in an 8-inch square greased baking dish, and sprinkle with half of the cheese. Next add the onion sauce, the shrimp, and the hard-boiled egg slices. Cover with the remaining spinach, sprinkle with the rest of the cheese, and bake in a moderate oven (300°F) for 30 minutes or until browned.

Yield: 4 to 6 servings

Heat Scale: Medium

A Matter of a *Piña*

"Like turkeys and avocado pears, pineapples have various names and nicknames in Spanish South America. In Venezuela, for instance, they are called (as in Cuba) *piñas* or 'pines.' In Brazil (in Portuguese), the usual word is *ananaz,* almost the same as the Spanish *ananás;* yet in Bahia they call it *abacashi*. We say, 'Don't be a prune, don't be a nut,' when we describe a liable soul. In Brazil they say, 'Don't be an *abacashi:* a pineapple.' "

—Charles Baker

Ensalada de Cerdo con Jalapeños

(Jalapeño Pork Salad)

In Latin America, pork is often treated with a generous squeeze of lime. In this Nicaraguan recipe, the citrus flavor serves as a wake-up call to the flavor of the meat and works well with the heat of the jalapeño.

2	pounds boneless pork butt or shoulder, cut into 1-inch cubes	½	cup finely chopped onion
½	cup water	3	or 4 fresh jalapeño chiles, seeds and stems removed, minced
	Salt and pepper	1½	quarts water
1	large tomato, cored	1	pound new potatoes, peeled and cut into ½-inch thick slices
2	tablespoons vegetable oil		Lime wedges
4	tablespoons lime juice		
3	cups finely shredded cabbage		

Place the pork in a 10- by 15-inch roasting pan. Add ½ cup water. Cover the pan tightly with aluminum foil and bake in a 400°F oven until meat is very tender when pierced, about 1 hour. Uncover and continue roasting, stirring occasionally, until all liquid evaporates, and meat is well browned, about 15 minutes longer. Add the salt and pepper to taste.

Meanwhile, while the meat cooks, cut 2 wedges from the tomato and dice the remainder. In a large bowl, combine the diced tomato, oil, 3 tablespoons lime juice, cabbage, and salt and pepper to taste; cover and chill. In a small bowl, mix the remaining 1 tablespoon of lime juice, onion, and chiles; cover and chill.

About 25 minutes before meat is finished cooking, bring about 1½ quarts water to boiling in a 3- to 4-quart pan. Add the potatoes, cover, and simmer until tender when pierced (potatoes may break apart slightly), 15 to 20 minutes; drain.

When meat is well browned, lift with slotted spoon onto a serving platter. Arrange the cabbage salad and hot potatoes alongside. Garnish with the tomato wedges. Serve the chile-onion salsa in a bowl with lime wedges for garnish.

Variation: Toss the pork with the salad and serve garnished with the potatoes.

Yield: 6 to 8 servings

Heat Scale: Medium

But What Time Do They Eat Breakfast?

"Except in the interior of Peru, *don't* invite Latins to tilt cocktails with you at five. For *por Díos, Señor!* at five your Latin male guest has barely quit the office before being chauffered home to siesta, shower, and change. He may show up at eight, but not before. And nine's better; figuring dinner by half-after ten! All right, we saw the daughter of the President of Uruguay walk into Cassoni's wonderful grill at 12:30 A.M., calm as you please, go to her reserved flower-laden table, and served the dinner—not supper—ordered for that precise hour."

—Charles Baker

Albóndigas con Ajís
(Ají Appetizer Meatballs)

Latin American meatballs are made with a variety of meats including beef, veal, or pork, and sometimes combinations of the three. This Uruguayan dish should be served with Salsa Criolla (p. 32) to add an interesting twist to this party food.

5	tablespoons vegetable oil	1	pound pork, finely ground
1	onion, minced	1	cup fresh bread crumbs
1	fresh ají chile, seeds and stem removed, chopped, or substitute yellow wax hot chiles	¼	cup grated Parmesan cheese
		¼	cup currants
1	tomato, peeled and chopped	½	teaspoon cinnamon
1	teaspoon light brown sugar	2	eggs, beaten
	Salt and freshly ground black pepper		Milk
			Flour

In a skillet, heat 2 tablespoons of the oil and sauté the onions until they are almost translucent. Add the chile, tomato, brown sugar, and salt and pepper to taste. Cook, stirring constantly, until the mixture is thick and dry. Remove the mixture from the heat and allow it to cool.

    In a bowl, combine the pork, bread crumbs, Parmesan cheese, currants, cinnamon, and the sautéed tomato mixture. Stir well. Add the eggs, mixing thoroughly. If the mixture is too dry add a little milk. Form the mixture into meatballs about 2 inches in diameter. Roll them in a small amount of flour. Heat the remaining oil in the skillet and fry the meatballs until they are lightly browned. As they are done, lift them out with a slotted spoon and drain them on paper towels. Serve the *albóndigas* with the Salsa Criolla.

Yield: 20 to 30 meatballs

Heat Scale: Mild

Butifarra

(Special Peruvian Sandwich)

The Incas were known to eat chiles with just about anything, "whether stewed, boiled, or roasted," and the tradition lives on today in Peru. This sandwich is a favorite at summertime fiestas.

½ cup grated onion

1 cup water with 3 tablespoons salt dissolved in it

¼ cup red wine vinegar

¼ cup grated fresh rocoto chiles, or substitute jalapeños

¼ cup diced radish

Salt and freshly ground black pepper to taste

1 tablespoon vegetable oil

1 lime, halved

12 bread rolls

12 lettuce leaves

12 slices roast beef

In a bowl, combine the onions and the salt water and mix well. Let stand for 1 minute, then drain off the salt water and add the vinegar. Keep the onions immersed in the vinegar until they acquire a rosy color. Next add the grated chiles, radish, salt, pepper, oil, and a little lime juice to the same container. Stir the mixture well, cover, and let sit in the refrigerator for 30 minutes.

Cut the rolls in half. Place a lettuce leaf and one slice of beef on each roll. Add the onion-chile sauce to top off the sandwich.

Yield: 12 sandwiches

Heat Scale: Medium

Bifes á la Criolla

(Brazilian Beef Creole)

This dish has deep black magic roots, as it is often served at ceremonies honoring Exu, the voodoo god who represents the middle man between the gods and the people.

½ cup olive oil
1½ pounds beef tenderloin, sliced ½-inch thick
4 potatoes, sliced
4 tomatoes, sliced
4 onions, sliced
5 fresh malagueta chiles, seeds and stems removed, chopped, or substitute piquins or red serranos

2 green bell peppers, seeds and stems removed, sliced
2 tablespoons chopped parsley
2 cloves garlic, minced
   Salt and freshly ground black pepper
1 cup beef stock

Heat the olive oil in a large covered skillet for 2 minutes, then remove from the heat and arrange layers of raw sliced beef, slices of thickly sliced potatoes, tomatoes, onions, malagueta peppers, green bell peppers, chopped parsley, garlic, and salt and pepper to taste. Repeat layers again. Add the meat stock and pour a little olive oil over the top. Cook on high heat, uncovered, for 10 minutes, then lower the heat and cook, covered, until the potatoes can be easily pierced with a fork, about 15 minutes.

Yield: 4 servings

Heat Scale: Medium

Torrejas de Maíz Tierno
(Fresh Corn Fritters)

These Colombian corn fritters are a wonderful accompaniment to any of the seafood dishes in Chapter 7. Try serving them with Pickapeppa Hot Sauce (p. 27) to really add an authentic Latin American flavor.

3 cups sweet corn, cut from the cob, with its liquid	1 large egg, lightly beaten
¼ cup flour	2 tablespoons grated cheddar cheese
2 tablespoons light brown sugar	¼ cup vegetable oil for frying
½ teaspoon salt	
1 teaspoon commercial habanero hot sauce	

Gently but thoroughly combine the corn and its liquid with the flour, sugar, salt, and hot sauce. Blend in the egg and cheese. Stir the batter well. Heat the oil to 265°F and drop in the batter by teaspoonfuls. Fry until golden brown on all sides. Drain on paper towels and serve very hot.

Yield: About 2 dozen 2-inch fritters

Heat Scale: Mild

Humitas Picantes

(Spicy Corn Casserole)

This Bolivian casserole (a large *tamal* without the wrapping) is served as a light first course. It is baked and then divided into squares and served on small elegant plates. It may also be used as a side dish for any of the poultry recipes in Chapter 6.

2	tablespoons chopped ají chiles, or substitute yellow wax hot chiles or red serranos	4	eggs
			Pinch of anise seed
			Salt, pepper, and sugar to taste
2	tablespoons vegetable oil	2	tablespoons raisins
2	cans cream-style corn	6	tablespoons flour

Sauté the chile in the oil for 5 minutes. In a separate bowl, mix together all the remaining ingredients, including the whole eggs. Stir in the chile mixture last. Mix well.

Pour the batter in a small casserole dish and bake at 400°F for 1 hour, or until done. Cut into squares immediately and serve on small plates.

Yield: 6 servings

Heat Scale: Medium

Humitas en Chala
(Seasoned Pureed Corn Tamales)

These light, little Chilean appetizers are especially wonderful served before a hearty meal such as the Arroz con Mariscos on p. 204.

3½ cups corn kernels (fresh or canned)

½ cup milk

1 teaspoon salt
Freshly ground black pepper

1 teaspoon ají chile powder, or substitute New Mexican

2 tablespoons margarine

1 onion, chopped

½ cup finely chopped summer squash

1 tablespoon chopped red bell pepper

1 tablespoon chopped fresh cilantro

¼ cup grated Parmesan cheese
Banana leaves (6 by 6 inches) or corn husks

Puree the corn kernels with the milk in a food processor. Add the salt, pepper, and chile powder and mix well. In a large frying pan, heat the margarine, and sauté the onion, squash, red bell pepper, and cilantro for 10 minutes. Add the pureed corn and cook, stirring continuously until it thickens, about 5 minutes. Add the grated cheese, mix well, and remove from heat.

Blanch the banana leaves or corn husks in boiling water and drain. One at a time, remove each husk and spread about 4 tablespoons of the corn mixture in the center of each husk. Fold the husk around the corn mixture to make a square packet, and tie securely with kitchen string. Make sure that all edges are sealed, and that no batter can escape from the husk. When all of the husks are filled, place them in a large pot of salted water to cover, and simmer on low heat, covered, for about 1 hour. Serve in their husks, warm. They can also be steamed.

Yield: 6 to 8 servings

Heat Scale: Mild

Nacatamales

(Nicaraguan Tamales)

This appetizer requires considerable advance preparation. However, the combination of the eclectic ingredients make it well worth the extra time. If you can locate the banana leaves, it is well worth the trouble as they really capture the authentic flavor of the dish. If not, corn husks will work fine. The quantity of these *nacatamales* is designed for serving at a large party.

3   cups white cornmeal
    Cold water
1   quart boiling water
6   tablespoons butter
3   teaspoons salt
2   large eggs, beaten well
4   cups diced lean raw beef
3   cups diced lean raw pork
3   cups diced raw chicken
2   cups cold water
3   small cloves garlic, minced or mashed
2   cups drained and coarsely chopped canned chick peas
⅓   cup olive oil
3   cups coarsely chopped ripe tomatoes
1   cup coarsely chopped green bell pepper

3   cups coarsely chopped onion
1   tablespoon ground cayenne
½   cup finely chopped fresh parsley
4   tablespoons cider vinegar
2   teaspoons sugar
3   teaspoons capers, coarsely chopped (optional)
¾   cup halved seedless raisins
¾   cup stuffed green olives, thinly sliced
⅓   cup crumbled fried bacon
2   cups corn kernels, cooked
1   cup tiny green peas, drained
½   cup diced pimientos, or substitute cooked red bell pepper
    Banana leaves, about 6 by 6 inches, or substitute corn husks

Combine the cornmeal with enough cold water to make a paste, then add this to a saucepan containing the 1 quart rapidly boiling water, stirring constantly. Add the butter and 2 teaspoons of the salt. Remove from heat and stir in the eggs until a smooth dough results. Reserve.

Meanwhile, in a large saucepan combine the beef, pork, chicken, 2 cups cold water, garlic, and the chick peas. Bring to a quick boil, then reduce heat and cook, stirring occasionally, until meats are tender. Drain well.

In a large skillet with a cover, heat the oil and add the tomatoes, green bell pepper, onion, cayenne, parsley, the remaining 1 teaspoon of salt, the vinegar, sugar, and the cooked meats. Cover and cook over low heat 15 minutes, stirring occasionally. Remove from the heat and gently stir in the capers, raisins, olives, bacon, corn, peas, and pimientos.

Blanch the banana leaves in boiling water and drain. Spread about 4 tablespoons of the dough mixture in the center of each banana frond, patting out to a thin layer. Place about 2 to 3 tablespoons of the meat-vegetable mixture on one side of the flattened dough, and roll the dough up carefully and tightly, sealing edges as thoroughly as possible with a little warm water or more dough, if needed. Fold the banana leaves around the *nacatamales* and tie them securely with kitchen string or thin strips of the banana leaves. Place in a large pot in salted water to cover, and simmer over very low heat, covered, about 1 hour. Serve *nacatamales* in their banana-leaf packets, hot or at room temperature, and open at the table.

Yield: 20 to 30 servings

Heat Scale: Medium

Empanadas de Nelly

(Nelly's Turnovers)

Empanadas, or meat-filled turnovers, are very popular throughout Latin America where they are most often eaten as a snack. These, from a recipe collected in Argentina by Susan Hazen-Hammond, were featured on the cover of *Chile Pepper* magazine.

Crust

1⅔ cups all-purpose flour

⅛ teaspoon salt

4 ounces stick butter or margarine

⅓ cup milk

Filling

1 pound ground beef

2 tablespoons vegetable oil, olive preferred

1 large onion, finely chopped

1 red bell pepper, seeds and stems removed, finely chopped

2 fresh ají chiles, seeds and stems removed, minced, or substitute yellow wax hot chiles or jalapeños

10 to 12 green olives, finely chopped

2 tablespoons raisins

1 tablespoon ground mild paprika

1 tablespoon chopped fresh parsley or substitute dried

1 medium potato, peeled, boiled, finely chopped

2 hard-boiled eggs, finely chopped

Salt and freshly ground black pepper to taste

Glaze

1 egg, beaten

1 tablespoon milk

To make the crust, sift the dry ingredients into a bowl. Work the margarine or butter into the flour using your fingers or two forks. Add the milk and mix just until the dough comes together and can be formed easily into a ball. Refrigerate for at least an hour.

Sauté the beef in a skillet until well done, stirring frequently with a fork to keep the meat broken up. In a separate skillet, heat the oil and sauté the onion, bell pepper, and chiles until the onions are a golden brown. Combine all of the filling ingredients in a large bowl and mix well.

Preheat the oven to 400°F.

Divide the dough in two and roll out to a thickness of ⅛-inch and cut into circles 7-inches in diameter. Spoon the filling onto one half of each, leaving room to fold in half, and seal. Press the edges with the tip of a fork and cut a 1-inch slice in the top. Place on an ungreased baking pan.

Combine the ingredients for the glaze.

Bake for 10 minutes. Reduce the heat to 350°F and continue baking until the crust turns light brown. Brush the tops with glaze and bake for an additional 5 minutes.

Yield: 10 empanadas

Heat Scale: Medium

Turnover Nomenclature

"One of the great food passions all South Americans share is for those tasty savory pastries called *empanadas, empadas, pasteles,* or, in Bolivia, *salteñas.* The word *empanada* is Spanish for 'breaded,' and it has come to mean a filled pastry turnover, patty, or pie. The average-size empanada yields about three handsome bites. Those consisting of just one bite are usually referred to as *empanaditas, pastelitos,* or *empadinhas,* though the diminutive is sometimes used more as a term of affection than description." —Felipe Rojas-Lombardi

Relleno de Queso Picante

(Spicy Cheese Filling)

This wonderful *empanada* filling is also from Argentina. The chiles give it just the right amount of bite. And speaking of bite, the expert *empanada* makers in Latin America advise that the perfect *empanada* can be consumed in a total of six small bites.

1½ cups ricotta cheese
    Salt
    Freshly ground white pepper
½ teaspoon paprika
½ teaspoon ají chile powder or substitute cayenne

4 scallions, chopped, including the greens
3 egg yolks, lightly beaten

Mix all the ingredients together. Chill slightly before using.

Yield: About 2 cups

Heat Scale: Medium

Recheio de Camarão

(Shrimp Stuffing, Bahian-Style)

This is another excellent *empanada* filling. It can also be served in puff pastry for an easy variation. Scallops may be substituted for the shrimp.

¼ cup vegetable oil

1 medium onion, finely chopped

1 medium green bell pepper, seeds and stem removed, and chopped

1 habanero chile, seeds and stem removed, chopped, or substitute 3 jalapeños

1 pound fresh shrimp, peeled, deveined, and chopped

Salt

Juice of 1 lime

½ cup palm hearts, chopped

2 egg yolks

½ cup thick coconut milk

1 tablespoon fresh cilantro, chopped

In a skillet, heat the oil and sauté the onion, bell pepper, and habanero until they are softened. Add the shrimp, salt to taste, juice of 1 lime, and palm hearts, and cook for 1–2 minutes. In a separate container, beat the egg yolks with the coconut milk and stir in the shrimp mixture. Add the cilantro and cook, stirring over low heat until the mixture has thickened. It should have the consistency of a medium white sauce. If necessary, thicken with ½ teaspoon arrowroot or cornstarch dissolved in 1 teaspoon water and cook for 1 or 2 minutes longer. Cool.

Yield: About 2 cups

Heat Scale: Hot

Andean Anticuchos

(Andean Shish Kebob with Hot Sauce)

Mary Dempsey, who wrote about Peru for *Chile Pepper*, commented: "*Anticucheros* are the street corner vendors who prepare the beef heart shish kebobs found all over Peru. Although the dish is spicy by itself, it would be unthinkable to eat anticuchos without spooning additional fiery chile sauce on top."

4   fresh ají chiles, seeds and stems removed, minced, or substitute red jalapeños
1   beef heart, nerves and fat removed and cut into large cubes (4 pounds of tender sirloin can be substituted)

1   cup vegetable oil
1   cup red wine vinegar
1   tablespoon ground cumin
    Salt and freshly ground black pepper to taste
    Salsa Picante de Peru (p. 17)

Combine all ingredients in a bowl (except the salsas) and marinate for 2 hours. Skewer the meat and grill it, turning the kebobs frequently, and brushing them twice again with the marinade, until done. Serve with Salsa Picante de Peru.

Yield: 8 servings

Heat Scale: Medium

And He Wasn't Bitter About the Career Change at All

In 1820, a German army surgeon, Dr. J. G. B. Siegert, arrived in Venezuela and set up a private medical practice on the banks of the Orinoco River. He soon became fascinated by the variety of medicinal herbs growing nearby, and started combining them in an attempt to make a remedy for stomach ailments. To enhance the aroma of the herbs and spices, he added some Venezuelan rum. By 1824, he had perfected his formula, which he sold under the name of "Angostura Aromatic Bitters." The bitters proved to be so popular that Siegert quit doctoring and devoted all his time to the enterprise that became the famous bitters—that are produced in Trinidad these days.

Anticuchos Picantes
(Spicier Grilled Beef Heart)

Peruvian people love really hot food. The marinade and sauce used with this version of *anticuchos* gives the dish a great big kick! Why not serve it with a Pisco Sour (p. 248)? This drink is very popular and makes a perfect addition to any barbecue.

1   beef heart

Marinade

6   to 8 cloves garlic, pressed
2   fresh rocoto chiles, seeds and stems removed, minced, or substitute red jalapeños
2   tablespoons ground cumin
½   tablespoon dried oregano, crumbled

Salt and freshly ground black pepper to taste
1½ to 2 cups red wine vinegar

Sauce

⅓   cup crushed dried ají chiles, or substitute New Mexican chiles
1   tablespoon vegetable oil
Salt to taste

Clean the beef heart thoroughly, removing all nerves and fat. Cut into 1-inch cubes and place the cubes into a non-reactive bowl. Refrigerate and set aside.

To make the marinade, combine the garlic, chiles, cumin, oregano, salt and pepper, and 1½ cups of the vinegar. Pour this over the meat. Add more vinegar, if necessary, to cover it completely. Marinate the meat in the refrigerator from 12 to 24 hours. Then, about 1 hour before grilling, remove the meat from the marinade and thread on skewers. Reserve the marinade.

For the sauce, soak the crushed chile in ⅓ cup warm water for 30 minutes. In a blender or food processor, combine the chiles and their water with the oil and salt. Add enough of the reserved marinade (about ¾ cup) to make a thick sauce, and puree.

Brush the skewered meat with the sauce and grill it over hot coals or under a broiler, turning and basting to cook quickly on all sides. The *anticuchos* are best cooked medium well, about 4 to 6 minutes on the grill, depending on the heat of the fire. Serve with the remaining sauce for dipping.

Note: This recipe requires advance preparation.

Yield: Serves 10 to 16

Heat Scale: Hot

Just What Every Bored, Rich Housewife Needs

"The wife of the sixth Inca had a thousand Indians as attendants, all of whom ate from the royal storehouse. She also had a thousand, or some say three thousand waiting women, who presumably also ate from the inexhaustible granaries. It was either her son or the son of the sixth Inca by some other wife who conquered the eastern slope of the Andes and brought back coca."
—Sophie D. Coe

Argentinean Anticuchos
(Skewered Spiced Sirloin)

The Argentine cowboys, or *gauchos,* are very proud of their beef but are not so proud that they won't borrow a recipe from neighboring Peru. This recipe is their version of *anticuchos,* but it is prepared with a better cut of meat. It is wise to soak the skewers in water for 30 minutes before using, which will prevent them from catching fire during grilling. Serve the kebobs with a salad and a robust red wine.

2　pounds sirloin, cut in 1½-inch cubes

　　Ground black pepper
1　tablespoon chopped cilantro

Marinade

1　cup vinegar
2　cloves garlic, crushed
3　dried ají chiles, crushed, or substitute New Mexican
1　teaspoon cumin seeds, crushed
1　teaspoon salt

Sauce

1　teaspoon Louisiana-style hot sauce
2　tablespoons tomato sauce
2　tablespoons vegetable oil
　　Freshly ground black pepper
1　teaspoon Worcestershire sauce

Place the sirloin in a bowl. Mix together all the marinade ingredients and pour over the sirloin cubes. If the marinade does not completely cover the meat, add more vinegar. Cover and refrigerate overnight. Remove the sirloin and reserve the marinade. Mix the sauce ingredients together and add ¾ cup of reserved marinade.

　　Thread the meat onto bamboo or wooden skewers and brush with the sauce. Cook over hot coals, or under a grill for about 4 to 6 minutes, depending on the heat of the fire, turning frequently and brushing with the sauce.

Yield: 6 servings

Heat Scale: Medium

4

Treinta Pucheros
30 Powerful Soups and Stews

S oups and stews are probably the most popular dishes in Latin America, and that's why we have so many of them in this chapter. Recipes for the Latin soups and stews are a dabbling cook's dream come true. Throughout Latin America, and some might say the entire world, people have been preparing these dishes with just what was available at the time—and often with spectacular results.

We find it amazing that a few changes here and there can completely alter the character of a recipe. The first four recipes in this chapter are perfect examples of a shared ingredient resulting in stunningly different flavors. Shellfish is the common theme running through these recipes. We have two versions of shrimp chowder. The first comes from Peru, Chupe de Camarones Numero Uno (p. 68), and is traditionally served with freshwater crayfish. The second, Chupe de Camarones Numero Dos (p. 70), is a popular chowder in Peru, Chile, and Ecuador. Its great taste is derived from the ground cashews, many spices, potatoes, rice, seafood—and of course, chiles! Chupe de Camarónes con Pescado (p. 72) is a delightful Peruvian shrimp and fish stew. The Moqueca de Camarão (Bahian Shrimp Stew, p. 73) is from Brazil and uses more basic ingredients and has an engaging texture.

As one might guess, fish stews are very popular and certainly very economical in the coastal areas of Latin America. We offer two recipes for Moqueca de Peixe. The first (p. 74) showcases the African influences of Brazil through the use of peppers and palm oil. The second version (p. 75) is quite spicy. Vatapá com Frutos do Mar (Brazilian Fish Stew, p. 76) is one of the most famous and most often prepared stews in Brazil. It is also an African-influenced recipe that includes peanuts, dried shrimp, and chiles.

You'll certainly gain a new and in-depth knowledge of potatoes after reading Chapter 8. Try Chupe de Camarones y Papas (Prawn and Yellow Potato Soup, p. 78) if you're already a fan of *papas*. You won't be disappointed.

Another great feature of soups and stews is that a little bit of meat goes a long way. This is especially important in many Latin American countries where meat is expensive. Since most soups and stews are a conglomerate of a variety of vegetables, spices, and other sundry items, they are thick and healthy, and may just have a hint of beef. Sopa de Lima (p. 80) is just such a meal. Although there is plenty of meat, the vegetables thicken and texturize the soup. Chupe Navideño de Bolivia (Bolivian Christmas Stew, p. 82) is a holiday favorite. We also offer Sancocho (Ecuadorian Beef Stew, p. 83). Puchero de Domingo (p. 84) is a spicy soup and main dish recipe collected by Susan Hazen-Hammond from relatives in Argentina. Lomo Saltado (Spicy Sirloin Stew, p. 86) features potato fries—trust us, it's wonderful!

Buy an extra pumpkin this October and plan to serve the Carbonada Criolla (p. 88) in it. This Argentinean stew combines a variety of fruits and vegetables, and looks great too.

Three types of smoked meat, black beans, and malagueta chiles are featured in Brazil's national dish, Feijoada Completa (p. 90). You'll need to get out your big stock pot for this one.

Next on our soup-stew adventure we encounter three pork stews and a pepperpot. Sancocho de Cerdo y Ají (Pepper Stew, p. 92) from Ecuador includes beer as an interesting ingredient. The Carne Guisado (Spicy Pork Stew, p. 93) from Guatemala is hot and savory. Sopa de Cerdo y Ajís (Pork and Chile Soup, p. 94) combines cilantro, ajís, and lime for a tangy treat from Bolivia.

The next stew is truly unique. The legend of Guyanese Pepperpot Soup (p. 95) allows that the stews were kept going for years, by adding ingredients each day. A main flavoring, cassareep, can be found in most Latin markets.

Last, but certainly not least, we've put together eleven vegetable based soups and stews. Locro de Ecuador (Vegetable Stew from Ecuador, p. 96) includes corn peppers, peas, and even pumpkins. But after that dish, things get wild! Porotos Granados (Grand Chile Stew, p. 97) features cranberries (they are available fresh year-round in Chile). And things would be most incomplete without at least two potato soup recipes: Ajiaco from Ecuador (p. 98), and Sopa de Camote Picante (p. 99) from Nancy Gerlach, are more than worthy Latin American representatives.

A mid-day meal is the perfect time to serve a light soup such as Sopa de Coco (Coconut Soup, p. 100). Sopa de Xim Xim (Peanut Soup, p. 101) is a much more stick-to-the-ribs kind of soup. Remember, a little bit of this soup goes a long way, in case you serve it as a first course rather than a main meal.

And to wind up the chapter, there is Sopa de Aguacate con Habanero (Habanero Avocado Soup, p. 102) from Guyana; Sopa de Quimbombó con Pescado (Piquant Okra and Pompano Soup, p. 103) from Colombia; and Cuchuco (Barley Soup, p. 00) from Uruguay. Don't forget to try Sopa de Ajo (Garlic Soup, p. 104) and Locro de Zapallo (Pumpkin Soup with Gruyère Cheese and Cumin, p. 106)—they're souper!

Chupe de Camarones Numero Uno

(Shrimp Chowder No. 1)

The "shrimp" most commonly served in Peru are actually freshwater crayfish whose tails turn bright red when cooked. North American shrimp are a good substitute in this recipe from *Chile Pepper*'s Nancy Gerlach.

1	medium onion, chopped	½	cup raw rice
2	cloves garlic, minced	2	cups whole kernel corn
2	to 3 tablespoons olive oil	1	pound raw shrimp, peeled and deveined
2	rocoto chiles, seeds and stems removed, chopped fine, or substitute jalapeños	1	cup half-and-half
2	teaspoons dried oregano		Salt and freshly ground black pepper to taste
1	large tomato, peeled and diced		Chopped fresh cilantro
1	quart chicken broth		

In a skillet or saucepan, sauté the onion and garlic in the oil until soft. Add the chiles, oregano, and tomato, and simmer for 5 minutes.

Transfer to a large kettle, and add the broth, rice, and corn. Bring to a boil, reduce the heat, and simmer for 25 minutes or until the rice is tender. Add the shrimp and simmer for an additional 5 minutes or until the shrimp is done.

Stir in the cream and season with salt and pepper. Garnish with cilantro and serve.

Yield: 4 to 6 servings

Heat Scale: Medium to Hot

Ecuadorian Heat

"I would rate Ecuadorian cuisine as only moderately hot. Although its heat is surely not a rival to East Indian or Thai cuisines, its consistent incorporation of *Capsicums* at every meal, coupled with the fact that this region has been using chile peppers for literally thousands of years longer than those formentioned cultures, makes Ecuadorian cuisine interesting to any chile enthusiast. The main source of heat for their meals is usually a bowl of freshly made picante sauce, or as Ecuadorians generally refer to it, *ají,* the generic term for chile pepper as well." —David Parrish

Chupe de Camarones Numero Dos

(Shrimp Chowder No. 2)

This dish has many versions—in at least three different countries—Peru, Chile, and Ecuador. Although it has many ingredients, it is still simple to prepare. After all, three Latin American countries can't be wrong.

6	scallions, including the green part, finely chopped	1	pound raw shrimp, peeled and deveined, reserve the shells
3	cloves garlic, minced	½	cup raw rice
¼	cup vegetable oil	3	medium potatoes, peeled and cut into quarters
3	tomatoes, peeled, seeded, and coarsely chopped	2	cups peas, fresh or frozen
3	rocoto chiles, seeds and stems removed, finely chopped or substitute jalapeños	2	ears corn, cut into 2-inch pieces
½	teaspoon nutmeg	1	pound firm white fish fillets, cut into bite-sized pieces
	Salt and freshly ground black pepper to taste	3	eggs, lightly beaten
3	quarts fish stock (or substitute chicken stock or part water and part clam juice)	1	cup evaporated milk or half-and-half, at room temperature
2	potatoes, peeled and coarsely chopped	3	tablespoons ground cashews

Sauté the scallions and the garlic in the oil until the onion is soft. Add the tomatoes, chiles, nutmeg, and the salt and pepper and cook for 2 to 3 minutes, stirring well. Add the stock, the chopped potatoes, and the shrimp shells and bring the mixture to a boil. Reduce the heat, cover, and simmer for 30 minutes.

Strain the stock through a sieve, pressing hard to extract as much of the solids as possible, or run it through a food mill (remove the shrimp shells first). Rinse the pan and return the stock to it.

Add the rice and the quartered potatoes, cover, and simmer until the potatoes and rice are done. Add the peas, corn, shrimp, and fish and simmer gently for 5 minutes. Do not boil or overcook at this point. With a fork, stir in the beaten eggs, allowing them to coagulate as threads. Add the milk and continue to simmer just long enough to heat through. Serve in soup bowls and sprinkle the ground cashews over the top.

Yield: 6 servings

Heat Scale: Mild

Early Incan T-Shirts

The Incas decorated bowls and dishes with chile pepper designs, and chiles also were the subject of embroidery designs. One example of textile art of the early Nazca period is a cotton cloth embroidered in yarn with twenty-three figures of farmers carrying their crops. One of the farmer figures is wearing chile pods around his neck and is carrying a plant bearing pods.

Chupe de Camarones con Pescado
(Shrimp and Fish Stew)

Because fish and shellfish are so plentiful in Peru, it is not surprising to find the two of them combined. This recipe takes a bit of time, but it is well worth it. The most important thing to remember is to be sure the stew doesn't boil, or the eggs will curdle.

2	tablespoons olive oil	2	teaspoons ají chile powder, or substitute New Mexican
1	onion, finely chopped		
2	whole cloves garlic	1	teaspoon marjoram
3	tablespoons tomato sauce	1	(3-ounce) package cream cheese
6	cups fish broth or use 3 cups clam juice and 3 cups water		
½	cup green peas	2	cups milk
½	cup corn	24	large shrimp, shelled and deveined
2	large potatoes, peeled and cubed	4	eggs, lightly beaten
1	teaspoon salt	6	small fillets of fried fish (sole, halibut, cod)

Heat the oil in a large saucepan and sauté the onion and garlic until nicely browned. Remove and discard the garlic cloves. Add the tomato sauce, fish broth, peas, corn, potatoes, salt, chile powder, and marjoram. Bring to a simmer and cook, covered, for 20 minutes. Beat the cream cheese until soft and add it bit by bit to the soup, stirring constantly. Stir in the milk, bring to a simmer, and add the shrimp. Cook 3 minutes and remove from the heat. Gradually add 2 cups of the hot soup to the eggs, stirring constantly. Pour the egg mixture back into the soup and reheat over low heat, stirring constantly. Place a piece of fried fish in each soup bowl, and ladle the soup over the fish.

Yield: 6 to 8 servings

Heat Scale: Medium

Moqueca de Camarão

(Bahian Shrimp Stew)

Brazil is famous for its delicious stews. However, stew in Brazil is not the same as the soup-like mixture we commonly associate with stew in the United States. In Brazil, a stew is often a thick mixture of ingredients served on a platter surrounded by an assortment of seafood, fruits, or vegetables. Serve this one with a green salad and French bread.

¼ cup olive oil
1 large onion, finely chopped
2 small carrots, peeled and thinly sliced
1 green bell pepper, seeds and stem removed, chopped
1 red bell pepper, seeds and stem removed, and chopped
4 medium tomatoes, peeled, seeded, and chopped

2 fresh malagueta chiles, seeds and stems removed, minced, or substitute piquins or red serranos
   Salt, freshly ground black pepper
2 pounds large shrimp, shelled and deveined
2 tablespoons vegetable oil

Heat the olive oil in a large, heavy skillet and sauté the onion, carrots, and green and red bell peppers until the onion is soft. Add the tomatoes, chiles, and salt and pepper to taste, and cook for a few minutes longer over moderate heat. Stir in the shrimp and the oil and cook, turning the shrimp once or twice, until the shrimp are pink and have lost their translucent color, about 3 minutes. Serve on a warmed platter.

Yield: 4 to 6 servings

Heat Scale: Medium

Moqueca de Peixe Número Uno

(Brazilian Moqueca No. 1)

Unlike other regions of Central and South America, Brazil had no great Indian civilization. Much of the cuisine of Brazil originated with the Portuguese and the slaves they brought from West Africa. Nowhere are these influences more evident than in the cooking of Bahia. This dish probably began as a mixture cooked in a banana leaf, and when the Europeans provided cooking pots, stews were born. A traditional meal includes white rice or a side of black beans, and okra with peanuts. A traditional malagueta sauce, such as Môlho Malagueta (p. 22), is served on the side to increase the heat.

1 habanero chile, seeds and stem removed, chopped, or substitute 3 jalapeños	3 tablespoons lime juice
1 bell pepper, stem and seeds removed, chopped	2 tablespoons palm oil, or substitute peanut oil with ½ teaspoon paprika
2 tomatoes, peeled and seeds removed, chopped	2 pounds fish fillets (sole, cod, haddock, or snapper)
1 onion, chopped	1 cup water
2 cloves garlic, chopped	Môlho Malagueta (see recipe p. 22) to taste
2 tablespoons chopped fresh cilantro	

Combine the chiles, bell pepper, tomatoes, onion, garlic, cilantro, and lime juice in a blender and puree until smooth. Sauté the sauce in 1 tablespoon of the oil for 10 minutes, stirring frequently.

Allow the sauce to cool, pour over the fish, and marinate for an hour.

Place the fish, marinade, the remainder of the oil, and a cup of water in a pan. Simmer the fish in the sauce until done, about 7 minutes. Serve sprinkled with Môlho Malagueta.

Yield: 4 servings

Heat Scale: Medium

Moqueca de Peixe Número Dos

(Brazilian Moqueca No. 2)

Here is another version of *moqueca* from Brazil. Since white fish is very mild, it soaks up the heat and fruitiness of the habanero to create a wonderful, wild stew.

3   pounds sole fillets, or any white fish, cut into 1-inch cubes

2   medium onions, chopped

2   fresh habanero chiles, seeds and stems removed, chopped, or substitute 6 jalapeños

3   medium tomatoes, peeled and chopped

1   clove garlic, chopped

2   tablespoons chopped cilantro
    Salt

4   tablespoons orange juice

½   cup cold water

¼   cup palm oil, or substitute vegetable oil mixed with ½ teaspoon paprika

Place the fish in a large bowl. In a blender or food processor combine the onions, habaneros, tomatoes, garlic, cilantro, salt to taste, and orange juice, and puree. Pour the puree over the fish, mixing lightly, and allow to stand for 1 hour. Transfer the fish and marinade to a saucepan. Add ½ cup cold water and ⅛ cup of palm oil. Cover and simmer until the fish is done, about 8 minutes. Pour the remaining ⅛ cup palm oil and cook just long enough to heat the oil through. Transfer the stew to a heated serving platter and surround with a border of plain white rice.

Yield: 6 servings

Heat Scale: Hot

Vatapá com Frutos do Mar

(Brazilian Fish Stew)

Vatapá is made with a variety of ingredients, ranging from fish to lean pork. Because there are so many variations among recipes, each version is as different as the cook who prepares it. This one includes peanuts, shrimp, and habaneros.

1 coconut, grated	1 lemon
Hot water	Salt
1 onion, sliced	1 pound fresh firm fish fillets, cut in 1-inch cubes
1 clove garlic	
2 fresh habanero chiles, seeds and stems removed, minced, or substitute 6 jalapeños	1 pound fresh shrimp, shelled and deveined
	1 cup ground roasted peanuts
1 bay leaf	½ pound dried shrimp, ground
1 tablespoon olive oil	Yellow cornmeal
7 cups water	2 tablespoons vegetable oil
1 lime	Sprigs of fresh cilantro

Spread the grated coconut on a baking pan. Sprinkle with a little hot water and set in a 350°F oven for 2 minutes to warm slightly. Place the coconut in 3 cups of hot water and let sit for 10 minutes. Squeeze the grated coconut through cheesecloth and reserve both the milk and gratings.

In a large stock pot, cook the onion, garlic, chiles, and bay leaf in the olive oil for a few minutes. Add 2 cups water and the juice of the lime and lemon. Season with salt and add sliced fish and shelled fresh shrimp. Cover and simmer until the fish is done, about 15 minutes. Remove the fish and shrimp and reserve. Strain the broth and set aside.

In a saucepan, add 5 cups water to the reserved coconut gratings and bring to a boil. Reduce the heat and simmer a few minutes. Strain, pressing out and reserving all liquid, but discarding the gratings. To this coconut broth add ground nuts and ground dried shrimp. Bring to a boil and cook until the nut and shrimp flavors have been extracted. Add strained broth from fish. Heat together and strain. Bring strained liquid to boiling point. Season with salt and stir in sufficient cornmeal to make a smooth, thick consistency. Cook over medium heat for 30 minutes, stirring frequently to prevent scorching. Add the cooked fish, cooked shrimp, and reserved coconut milk, heat through, then add 2 tablespoons oil. Serve in soup bowls garnished with the cilantro. The consistency of this dish should be that of thick cream.

Yield: 6 to 8 servings

Heat Scale: Hot

From Feast to Fast

"They [Indians] call it *uchu,* and the Spaniards say *pimento de las Indias,* though in America it is called *ají,* a word from the language of the Windward Islands. The inhabitants of my own country [Peru] are so attached to *uchu* that they will eat nothing without it, even for instance a few uncooked herbs. Because of the pleasure they obtain from it, they used to prohibit the eating of it when they were observing a strict fast."

—Garcilaso de la Vega (El Inca)

Chupe de Camarones y Papas

(Prawn and Yellow Potato Soup)

There are more than 200 varieties of potatoes available in Peru. They are grown by just about every household and are consumed at most meals. The mixed seafood in this dish is also typical of Peru.

2 tablespoons vegetable oil
½ cup chopped onion
1 clove garlic
2 tablespoons tomato sauce
8 cups water
½ cup green peas
1 cup uncooked corn kernels
2 pounds yellow potatoes, peeled, chopped, and boiled until tender
2 teaspoons ají chile powder, or substitute New Mexican
1 can (6 to 8 ounces) crab meat

1 dozen prawns, or substitute large shrimp, peeled and deveined
½ teaspoon marjoram
Salt and pepper to taste
2 cups milk
½ cup grated Monterey jack cheese
4 eggs, slightly beaten
4 fillets halibut or other white fish, halved
Vegetable oil

Place the oil in a casserole dish, heat, and sauté the onion and garlic, removing the garlic when brown. Add the tomato sauce, 1 cup of water, green peas, and the corn and cook 10 minutes. Add remaining water, potatoes, chile powder, crab meat, prawns, marjoram, salt, pepper, milk, cheese, and the eggs. Cook, uncovered, for 10 minutes.

Fry the fish in a little oil, and just before serving the soup, add the fillets. Serve hot.

Yield: 8 to 10 servings

Heat Scale: Medium

A Stew by Any Other Name . . .

"One type of soup found in every South American country, though the name and traditional ingredients vary from place to place, is what in North America is called a boiled dinner. Meat, poultry, fish, and/or sausages are cooked in water or stock with vegetables. In Peru this is called *sancochado;* in Ecuador and Colombia, *sancocho;* in Venezuela, *hervido;* in Chile, *cazuela,* after the earthenware pot in which it is cooked; in Brazil, *cozido,* and in Argentina, Uruguay, Paraguay, and Bolivia, *puchero.* When *puchero* is made with sausages in Uruguay, it is called *olla podrida,* literally "rotten pot," and it is delicious despite its name."

—Felipe Rojas-Lombardi

Sopa de Lima

(Lima Soup)

This soup is a favorite in Lima, the capital of Peru. It is different from the Yucatecan soup of the same name. The rocoto, the featured chile in this recipe, was a principal crop of the Inca society in Peru, and centuries later is still the chile of choice. Cooks will have to grow their own or substitute jalapeños; however, persons living near the Mexican border can often find the rocoto's close relatives, called *canarios,* in markets in cities such as Ciudad Juárez.

4   quarts water (or more if necessary)

2   pounds beef brisket, flank, or short ribs

1   whole onion

1   whole tomato

½   cup dried chick peas

1   small cabbage
    Bouquet garni: 2 sprigs parsley, 1 sprig fresh rosemary, 2 sprigs fresh thyme, 4 whole black peppercorns, all tied in cheese-cloth

1   whole rocoto or jalapeño chile

1   teaspoon salt

6   carrots, cut into ½-inch pieces

3   turnips, peeled and cut into ½-inch cubes

2   ears corn, cut into 2-inch rounds

1   small yuca (cassava), peeled and cut into ½-inch cubes (optional)

3   potatoes, cut into ½-inch cubes

1   cabbage, cut into eighths

3   leeks, white part only, sliced into ½-inch pieces

1   celery rib

Sauce

1   tablespoon cooking oil

1   cup sliced onion

½   cup sliced rocoto chiles, or substitute jalapeños
    Salt and pepper to taste

Heat the water in a large, deep casserole or stock pot. When the water is warm, add the beef, onion, tomato, chick peas, and the bouquet garni. Bring the water to a boil, reduce heat, and simmer briskly for ½ hour.

Remove the onion and tomato, press through a fine sieve, and return the puree to the pot. Add the whole chile and cook for an additional 1½ hours.

Add the salt, carrots, turnips, corn, yuca (if using), potatoes, cabbage, leeks, and celery and simmer until the vegetables are tender, 20 to 30 minutes.

Remove the meat to a platter and remove the vegetables with a slotted spoon and arrange them around the meat. Keep warm in the oven.

Heat the oil and sauté the onion and sliced chiles until the onion is translucent. Add salt and pepper to taste.

Serve the broth in soup bowls first, followed by the meat and vegetables covered with the sauce.

Yield: 6 to 8 servings

Heat Scale: Varies, but probably medium

The Higher You Go In Peru, the Hotter You Get

"Even in the jungle, where food tends not to burn the palate, Amazon residents routinely dip jungle vegetables and *yucca* into fiery sauces. But the hottest of all foods, the plates that ignite the faces of their eaters, get noses running and bring tears to the eyes, come from the highlands. Here, picante, as the hot spiciness is known, reaches an art form." —Mary Dempsey

Chupe Navideño de Bolivia

(Bolivian Christmas Stew)

Holidays are important times in this Roman Catholic country. This soup is a traditional meal served during the Advent season. For an exciting mix of Latin American cuisines, serve Rompope (Ecuadorian Eggnog, p. 247) as a dessert drink.

2	medium onions, chopped	1	teaspoon chopped fresh parsley
1	medium tomato, chopped	1	tablespoon chopped fresh ají chile, or substitute yellow wax hot chiles or jalapeños
4	teaspoons vegetable oil		
1	medium chicken, cut up		
1	pound pork loin, cut into 1-inch cubes	½	cup cherry wine
	Water to cover	½	cup peas
1	teaspoon oregano		Freshly ground black pepper
1	teaspoon salt		Parsley and hard-boiled eggs for garnish

Sauté the onions and tomato in oil for a few minutes in a large pan. Add the chicken and pork and brown lightly. Add water to cover, then add remaining ingredients, except the wine, peas, black pepper, and garnishes. Bring to a boil, reduce heat, cover, and cook over low heat for 50 minutes. Add the peas, wine, and pepper to taste. Let cook 10 minutes more or until peas are tender. Serve with white rice and garnish with fresh parsley and sliced hard-boiled eggs.

Yield: 6 to 8 servings

Heat Scale: Medium

Sancocho

(Ecuadorian Beef Stew)

This stew features pineapple, whose name comes simply from the fact that it is cone-shaped. The tender beef, vegetables, fruit, and chiles combine well for a tangy, spicy taste.

2   whole cloves garlic
3   tablespoons butter
1   large onion, chopped
2   tomatoes, chopped
2   fresh ají chiles, seeds and stems removed, chopped, or substitute yellow wax hot chiles or jalapeños
4   cups fresh pineapple, chopped into bite-sized pieces
1   green bell pepper, chopped
1½ pounds lean beef cut into 1-inch cubes

Salt and freshly ground black pepper to taste
1   teaspoon sugar
3   white potatoes, peeled and diced
3   sweet potatoes, peeled and diced
6   ears corn, kernels cut whole off the cob
1½ cups beef broth or consommé

Fry the garlic in the butter and when it is well-browned remove and discard. Add chopped onion, fry for a few minutes, then add the tomatoes, chiles, pineapple, bell pepper, beef, salt, pepper, and sugar. Let cook for 15 minutes, then add the potatoes and sweet potatoes. Stir, lower the heat, and add the corn and beef broth. Simmer for 40 minutes, adding more broth if the mixture becomes too dry.

Yield: 6 to 8 servings

Heat Scale: Medium

Puchero de Domingo
(Domingo's Spicy Meat Soup)

Susan Hazen-Hammond collected this recipe from relatives in Argentina. She wrote in *Chile Pepper:* "This one-pot dish is served as two courses. Traditionally, each diner mashes the vegetables with a fork and sprinkles them with lemon juice (or vinegar), olive oil, salt, and pepper. Following the main course, the broth is reheated and served as a soup."

3 to 4 tablespoons vegetable oil, olive preferred

4 onions, 2 finely chopped, 2 whole

2 red bell peppers, stems and seeds removed, finely chopped

2- to 3-pound chuck roast, cut in 4 to 6 pieces

3 to 4 quarts water

1 head cabbage, cut in half

2 yams, peeled, cut in half

8 medium carrots, peeled

4 potatoes, peeled

1 acorn squash, peeled and quartered

2 whole ají p-p chiles, or substitute piquins (or more, to taste)

   Salt and freshly ground black pepper to taste

2 ears fresh corn, broken in half

   Lemon juice and olive oil for garnish

Heat the oil in a large pot and sauté the chopped onions and bell peppers until soft. Add the beef, 2 quarts of water, cover and simmer over low heat for 2 hours.

Add the cabbage, whole onions, yams, carrots, potatoes, squash, chile, and salt and pepper, and continue to simmer for 45 minutes, adding more water as needed. Add the corn and cook 20 minutes more.

Remove the chiles and discard. Remove the meat and vegetables and reserve the broth. Cut the whole onions in half.

Place the beef on individual plates and surround it with the vegetables. Serve with lemon juice and olive oil on the side. Following the main course, reheat broth and serve as a soup.

Yield: 4 to 6 servings

Heat Scale: Mild

Lomo Saltado

(Spicy Sirloin Stew)

This Peruvian stew is from Mary Dempsey, who commented: "Sirloin strips, potatoes, onions, and tomatoes are the basic ingredients of this dish—but the touch that makes it memorable is the pepper spicing." And that, of course, calls for exotic chiles. In Peru, this dish is served with rice. Jicama and Orange Salad (p. 38) is a good complement.

4   yellow or new potatoes, peeled
¼   cup vegetable oil for frying
1   pound sirloin steak, cut in strips
2   large onions, sliced
1   clove garlic, minced
2   large tomatoes, cut into thin wedges

3   fresh ajís, seeds and stems removed and cut into strips, or substitute yellow wax hot chiles, or red jalapeños
½   cup chopped parsley or cilantro
¼   cup wine or vinegar
    Salt and freshly ground black pepper to taste

Cut the potatoes into strips, as for french fries, and fry them in the oil in a large skillet until golden. Remove, drain, and set aside the fries and pour out all but 2 tablespoons of the cooking oil. In the same pan, over medium heat, brown the meat, then add the onions, garlic, tomatoes, chiles, parsley, wine or vinegar, and the salt and pepper. Sauté until the onion is soft, then cover and cook 15 more minutes. Add the potatoes and serve immediately (so the fries do not become soggy).

Yield: 4 servings

Heat Scale: Medium

And That Would Seriously Impair One's Craving for Brazil Nuts

"When growing on the tree the [Brazil] nuts are contained in large, almost spherical or slightly pear-shaped woody capsules, each filled with from eighteen to twenty-five nuts closely fitted together in regular tiers. As one of these big fruits may weigh five or six pounds it is far from safe to walk or sit beneath one of the trees when the nuts are ripe and ready to fall. Such a missile, dropping for sixty or seventy feet or even less, is about as deadly as a cannonball and will easily crush a man's skull." —A. Hyatt Verrill

Carbonada Criolla

(Creole Stew of Beef, Squash, and Peaches)

There are as many variations of this recipe as there are cooks in Argentina! For a party, you might want to serve the stew in a pumpkin or squash shell, but you must be very careful that the shell doesn't get too soft or the stew will collapse it and create a map of Argentina on your table. Argentine stews frequently contain several varieties of fruits and vegetables, along with the meat. And the choice of meat would, of course, be beef from the expansive pampas.

1	10- to 12-pound pumpkin
2	to 3 tablespoons olive oil
4	pounds beef chuck or rump, cut into 1-inch cubes
2	medium onions, coarsely chopped
1	large green bell pepper, seeds and stem removed, chopped
2	cloves garlic, minced
4	cups fresh or canned beef stock
2	large tomatoes, peeled, seeded, and coarsely chopped
1	teaspoon salt
½	teaspoon freshly ground black pepper

2	teaspoons sugar
2	tablespoons chopped cilantro
1	bay leaf
½	teaspoon oregano
½	teaspoon thyme
3	ají p-p chiles, stems removed, crushed, or substitute piquins
1½	pounds sweet potatoes, peeled and cut into ½-inch cubes
3	ears corn, cleaned, and cut into 1½-inch rounds
3	fresh peaches, peeled, pitted, and halved, or substitute frozen, thawed, and drained

Clean the outside of the pumpkin under running water. Cut off the top of the pumpkin to make a lid, making the opening 6- to 8-inches in diameter and clean out the inside. Replace the lid and bake the pumpkin in a roasting pan at 350°F for 20 minutes.

Heat the olive oil in a large casserole and add the cubed meat, a little at a time, and brown the meat on all sides. As the meat browns, remove it to an 8-quart heavy Dutch oven. To the remaining oil in the casserole, add the onion, green pepper, and garlic and sauté the mixture until the onion softens. Add the sautéed mixture to the browned meat. Add the beef broth and bring this mixture to a boil.

Add the tomatoes, salt, pepper, sugar, cilantro, bay leaf, oregano, thyme, and the crushed chile. Reduce the heat, cover, and simmer for 1½ hours, stirring occasionally.

Add the cubed sweet potatoes and cook, covered, for 15 minutes. Finally, add the corn and the peaches and cook, covered, for an additional 10 minutes.

Carefully ladle the beef mixture into the pumpkin shell, replace the lid, and bake the filled pumpkin on a large, shallow roasting pan at 325°F for 45 minutes, checking to make sure that the shell is not getting too soft.

If you are a brave soul, you can remove the filled pumpkin to a large platter. Or, if you are normal, you can leave the filled pumpkin in the pan and decorate the pan with Indian corn and sprigs of dried, colored leaves. As you serve the stew, scrape off parts of the inside of the pumpkin, too.

Yield: 8 servings

Heat Scale: Medium

Feijoada Completa

(Brazilian Black Bean Stew)

This stew is so popular it is thought of as the national dish of Brazil. It features smoked meats and the Brazilian favorite, black beans. To serve this stew without black beans would be sacrilege to a Brazilian! The smoked tongue and carne seca are available in Latin markets, but feel free to substitute other smoked meats.

1	smoked beef tongue	2	onions, finely chopped
2	pounds black beans, soaked overnight and drained	2	cloves garlic, crushed
2	pounds carne seca (dried beef), soaked overnight and drained	2	tomatoes, peeled, seeded, and chopped
2	pounds *linguiça* (seasoned Brazilian pork sausage), or substitute Chorizo (p. 126)	2	bay leaves
½	pound bacon, in one piece	3	fresh malagueta chiles, seeds and stems removed, minced, or substitute piquins or red serranos
½	pound smoked loin of pork	2	tablespoons finely chopped parsley
½	pound salt pork, cubed	4	oranges, peeled and sliced
2	tablespoons vegetable oil		

Place the tongue in a large pan and add water to cover. Bring to a boil, lower the heat and simmer, covered, 2½ hours until tender. Drain and remove the skin and any gristle when the tongue is cool enough to handle. Place the beans, carne seca, *linguica,* bacon, pork loin, and salt pork in a very large casserole. Add cold water to cover. Bring to a boil, lower the heat and simmer, covered, 1 hour. Check occasionally to see if the liquid is being absorbed too quickly by the beans. Add boiling water as necessary to keep the ingredients barely covered. Add the tongue and continue cooking 1 hour until the beans are tender.

Heat the oil in a skillet and sauté the onions and garlic until soft. Add the tomatoes, bay leaves, chile, and parsley and simmer for 5 minutes. Remove about 2 cups of the black beans from the casserole with a slotted spoon and mash them into the onion-tomato mixture. Cook, stirring constantly, about 2 minutes. Remove and slice the meats. Arrange them on a large platter with the tongue in the center. Garnish with orange slices. Add the thick bean sauce to the remaining black beans in the casserole. Cook, stirring, about 2 minutes. Place the beans in a soup tureen. Serve the *feijoada* with rice, greens, and Môlho com Pimenta e Limão (p. 23).

Yield: 10 to 12 servings

Heat Scale: Medium

Sancocho de Cerdo y Ají

(Pepper Stew)

Ecuador is home to more than thirty volcanoes. With the added heat of the ají chiles, this stew is as hot as the country.

2 tablespoons cooking oil	1 tablespoon coarsely chopped cilantro
3 pounds lean pork shoulder, cut in 1-inch cubes	½ teaspoon ground cumin
1 onion, finely chopped	½ teaspoon oregano
2 cloves garlic, minced	Salt and freshly ground black pepper
1 tomato, peeled, seeded, and chopped	Pinch of sugar
1 red bell pepper, seeded and coarsely chopped	2 cups beer
5 fresh ají chiles, seeds and stems removed, finely chopped, or substitute yellow wax hot chiles or jalapeños	

Heat the oil in a heavy skillet and lightly sauté the pork cubes. With a slotted spoon remove the pork pieces to a casserole. Remove all but 2 tablespoons of fat from the skillet, add the onion and garlic, and sauté the mixture until the onion is soft. Add the tomato, the bell pepper, chile, cilantro, cumin, and oregano, and simmer until the mixture is well blended, about 10 minutes. Season to taste with salt and pepper and the pinch of sugar. Pour over the pork in the casserole, add the beer, cover, and cook over very low heat until the pork is tender, about 2 hours. The sauce should be very thick. If it seems at all watery, partially uncover the casserole during the second hour of cooking. Serve with rice.

Yield: 6 to 8 servings

Heat Scale: Hot

Carne Guisado

(Spicy Pork Stew)

This dish is from Guatemala, which is situated between the Pacific Ocean and the Caribbean Sea. Agriculture is a main industry of the country. The use of spices and sour orange juice shows the Caribbean influence on Guatemalan cuisine.

2	tablespoons vegetable oil	1	cinnamon stick, 1-inch long
2	pounds pork, cut into 1-inch cubes	1	teaspoon nutmeg
½	teaspoon salt, or to taste	3	cups water
½	teaspoon freshly ground black pepper	¼	cup sour orange juice, or substitute half orange juice, half lime juice
3	bay leaves	½	cup sliced ripe tomato
¼	teaspoon thyme	2	tablespoons minced onion
⅛	cup minced jalapeños, or substitute ¼ cup minced roasted and peeled New Mexican green chiles	1	clove garlic, sliced
		¼	cup toasted bread crumbs

Heat the oil in a saucepan over moderate heat and brown the pork for 5 minutes. Sprinkle with salt, pepper, bay leaves, thyme, chile, cinnamon, and nutmeg. Stir well, add the water and orange juice, and bring to a boil. Reduce the heat to a simmer.

Combine the tomato, onion, and garlic in a blender and puree. Add this to the pork and continue to simmer for about 1 hour, or until pork is tender.

Add the crumbs to thicken the sauce, and simmer over low heat for 10 minutes more. If the sauce has thickened too much, add ¼ cup more water. Serve hot.

Yield: 6 servings

Heat Scale: Medium

Sopa de Cerdo y Ajís
(Pork and Chile Soup)

Bolivians enjoy their cuisine *muy picante*. The high altitude and cold evenings make soups and stews (along with a little chile) appropriate in any season. This particular dish is simple and delicious and features pork, ajís, and, of course, potatoes.

1	tablespoon oil	2	cloves garlic, crushed
2	pounds boneless lean pork, cubed	5	cups water
1	large onion, sliced	4	medium potatoes, peeled and quartered
1	teaspoon ground cumin	2	cups corn kernels
2	teaspoons salt	2	tablespoons green bell pepper, chopped
	Freshly ground black pepper	¼	cup lime juice
2	dried ají chiles, crushed, or substitute New Mexican		Chopped cilantro for garnish

Heat the oil in a large saucepan and brown the pork. Add the onion, cumin, salt, pepper, and chiles and stir for 2 minutes. Add the garlic and the water, cover and simmer for 30 minutes. Add the potatoes and continue cooking until they are tender, about 20 minutes. Mix in the corn kernels, bell pepper, and lime juice and simmer for 10 minutes. Check the seasoning and ladle into soup bowls. Sprinkle fresh, chopped cilantro over each serving.

Yield: 6 servings

Heat Scale: Medium

Guyanese Pepperpot Soup

Food historians believe that this dish originated in Guyana and was later spread throughout the West Indies by the Arawak Indians. The key ingredient is cassareep, which is the boiled-down juice of raw cassava. It is available bottled in Latin markets (and some Asian markets), or by mail order. Legend holds that in the early days, a pepperpot was always in the kitchen, and more ingredients were added to it each day, keeping the pot going for years.

2	beef marrow bones, washed	½	cup cassareep
1	pound beef, cut into 1-inch cubes		Water to cover
1	pound pork, cut into 1-inch cubes		Salt and freshly ground black pepper to taste
2	onions, chopped		
2	whole habanero chiles, tied in a cheesecloth bag, or substitute 6 jalapeños		

Place the meats in a stew pot, add the onions, chiles, cassareep, and water to cover. Bring to a boil, reduce heat, and simmer until the meats are tender and nearly falling apart, about 2 hours.

Remove the marrow bones and the habaneros and serve.

Yield: 6 to 8 servings

Heat Scale: Medium

Locro de Ecuador

(Vegetable Stew from Ecuador)

This stew is a perfect summer dish for the numerous vegetables grown in home gardens. *Locros* are thick stews famous for the many vegetables used in them. The addition of the pumpkin and Gruyère cheese gives it a unique flavor.

2	tablespoons butter	1	cup fresh or frozen peas
2	onions, finely chopped	1	teaspoon salt
2	cloves garlic, minced		Freshly ground black pepper
½	cup tomato sauce	4	medium–sized potatoes, peeled and cut into eighths
½	cup water		
1	cup canned corn, drained	1	can (16 ounces) pumpkin
2	fresh ají chiles, seeds and stems removed, chopped, or substitute yellow wax hot chiles or jalapeños	1	cup milk
		¾	cup grated Gruyère cheese

Heat the butter in a large saucepan and sauté the onions and garlic until golden brown. Add the tomato sauce, water, corn, chile, peas, salt and pepper and bring to a boil. Lower the heat, cover, and simmer 10 minutes. Add the potatoes, pumpkin, and milk. Cover and simmer over the lowest possible heat for 45 minutes to 1 hour. Stir in the cheese and remove from the heat. Serve with rice.

Yield: 6 to 8 servings

Heat Scale: Medium

Porotos Granados

(Grand Chile Stew)

This stew is the national dish of Chile. It should be served with Pebre sauce (p. 18). *Porotos* is the Indian word for fresh cranberry beans. They are available year-round in Chile, but we suggest substituting navy beans.

1½ cups dried cranberry beans, or substitute navy beans
   Water
1 large onion, coarsely chopped
4 ají chiles, seeds and stems removed, chopped, or substitute yellow wax hot chiles or jalapeños
4 tablespoons olive oil
1 clove garlic, minced
6 tomatoes, peeled, seeded, and chopped

½ teaspoon basil
1½ teaspoons oregano
½ teaspoon thyme
   Salt and freshly ground black pepper to taste
2 cups winter squash (about 1 pound), peeled and cut into ½-inch cubes
⅓ cup corn kernels

Cover the beans with cold water, bring to a boil, turn off the heat, and allow the beans to soak for 1 hour. Change the water, bring the beans to a boil again, reduce the heat, and simmer for 1 hour.

In a large skillet, sauté the onion and chile in the oil until it is soft. Add the garlic, tomatoes, basil, oregano, thyme, salt and pepper, and cook, stirring over medium heat until the mixture forms a thick puree. Set aside.

When the beans have cooked for 1 hour and are almost tender, add the tomato puree and the squash and continue cooking until the beans are completely done and the squash is mushy. Stir in the corn and cook for an additional 5 minutes.

Yield: 6 servings

Heat Scale: Hot

Ajiaco

(Ecuadorian Potato Soup)

In Latin America, nearly every meal begins with soup. The unique ingredients in this dish are the cream cheese and avocados, which make for a rich, smooth texture that slides over the palate, leaving in its wake a touch of the heat of the ajís.

4	tablespoons butter	1	teaspoon ají chile powder, or substitute cayenne
3	onions, finely chopped		
2	tablespoons flour	3	cups milk
3	cups chicken broth	½	cup fresh green peas
4	potatoes, peeled and diced	3	eggs
⅛	teaspoon saffron	¼	pound cream cheese
1½	teaspoons salt	1	avocado, peeled and sliced

Heat the butter in a large saucepan. Add the onions and sauté for 10 minutes. Add the flour and mix until smooth. Add the chicken broth gradually, stirring constantly until boiling. Add the potatoes, saffron, salt, and chile powder and simmer for 20 minutes.

Add the milk and peas and continue cooking gently for 5 minutes. Beat the eggs and cream cheese together in a bowl and gradually add 2 cups of the hot soup, beating constantly to avoid curdling. Return the contents of the bowl to the saucepan and heat but do not boil. Place a few thin slices of avocado in each soup bowl and pour the hot soup over them.

Yield: 6 servings

Heat Scale: Medium

Sopa de Camote Picante

(Spicy Sweet Potato Soup)

Here is Nancy Gerlach's version of a soup from Arlene Lutz that we were served in Escazú, Costa Rica. We took the liberty of adding some habanero powder to spice it up. Arlene's secret is to add a little sugar if the potatoes are not sweet enough.

4	cups chicken broth	½	teaspoon habanero chile powder, or substitute cayenne
2	cups diced sweet potato		Pinch of white pepper
3	tablespoons orange juice		Chopped parsley for garnish
¼	teaspoon orange zest		
3	tablespoons heavy cream		

In a soup pot, bring the broth to a boil, add the potatoes and boil until they are soft. Place the potatoes and some of the broth in a food processor or blender and puree the mixture until smooth.

Combine the puree with the reserved broth and the remaining ingredients. Simmer for 20 minutes.

Garnish with the parsley and serve.

Yield: 4 servings

Heat Scale: Medium

Sopa de Coco
(Coconut Soup)

This recipe hails from the tropical lowlands of the Republic of Colombia, where coconuts are frequently used in cooking. Tortillas cut into strips are a nice accompaniment.

2　large ripe coconuts, cracked, meat grated

2　cups milk, scalded

3　cups strained fish stock, or substitute chicken stock

2　egg yolks, well beaten

½　habanero chile, seeds and stem removed, minced, or substitute 1½ jalapeños

Paprika to taste

Salt to taste

Combine the grated coconut and the milk. Let cool, then squeeze through cheesecloth or a linen napkin to extract all the liquid. Combine the coconut milk, stock, egg yolks, and chile in a saucepan and cook for 10 minutes, stirring constantly.

To serve, sprinkle with paprika and salt to taste, and accompany with strips of toast or tortillas.

Yield: 4 servings

Heat Scale: Medium

Sopa de Xim Xim

(Peanut Soup)

Peanut soup is the traditional dish of the Afro-Brazilian community, who quickly adopted this New World food. This rich, thick soup is wonderful accompanied by Corn Fritters (p. 51).

1	pound stewing beef, cut into 1-inch cubes
6	cups cold water
4	beef bouillon cubes
1	onion, finely chopped
¼	teaspoon salt
	Freshly ground black pepper
1	cup peanut butter

1	green bell pepper, seeded and chopped
2	red bell peppers, seeded, cut into strips
1	habanero chile, seeds and stem removed, minced, or substitute 3 jalapeños

Place the beef, water, bouillon cubes, onion, salt and pepper in a saucepan and bring to a boil. Lower the heat, cover, and simmer for 1½ to 2 hours until the beef is tender. Place the peanut butter in a bowl and gradually add 1 cup of the broth, stirring until the peanut butter is dissolved. Add the peanut butter mixture back to the soup, a little at a time, stirring constantly. Add the green pepper, red pepper, and habanero and simmer, uncovered, 15 minutes. Stir well and serve.

Yield: 6 servings

Heat Scale: Hot

Sopa de Aguacate con Habanero
(Habanero-Avocado Soup)

Guyana is the only English speaking country situated in South America. The avocado is a rich gift of that land; however, it must be treated carefully. Make sure you don't cook the avocado, or the soup will turn bitter.

2   large, ripe avocados, peeled and pitted

1   habanero chile, seeds and stem removed, minced, or substitute 3 jalapeños

4   cups rich chicken stock

1   cup heavy cream

Salt and freshly ground white pepper

1   tablespoon cilantro, finely chopped

6   tortillas, quartered and fried crisp in oil

Mash the avocados and put them through a sieve. Place them in a heated soup tureen. Heat the habanero and chicken stock with the cream in a saucepan and stir well. Pour the stock into the avocados, stirring to mix, or beat lightly with a wire whisk. Season to taste with salt and pepper. Sprinkle with the cilantro. Serve immediately with the crisp tortillas.

Yield: 4 to 6 servings

Heat Scale: Hot

Sopa de Quimbombó con Pescado

(Piquant Okra and Pompano Soup)

Both the cuisine and the land of Colombia are rich—more than half of the world's emeralds are produced in Colombia. As with many gumbos, this soup is thickened with okra, enlivened with chiles, and delicious to eat.

2	quarts fish stock	½	pound small, fresh okra, quartered
2	medium onions, finely chopped		
2	cloves garlic, chopped	1	pound small yams, peeled and cut into 1-inch cubes
1	large tomato, peeled, seeded, and chopped		
		2	ripe plantains, peeled and sliced
2	habanero chiles, seeds and stems removed, chopped, or substitute 6 jalapeños	2	tablespoons butter
		6	pompano fillets
		2	tablespoons tomato paste
¼	teaspoon ground cumin	1	tablespoon Worcestershire sauce
¼	teaspoon allspice		
	Salt		Salt and freshly ground black pepper
4	tablespoons lemon juice		

In a stock pot, combine the fish stock, onions, garlic, tomato, habaneros, cumin, and allspice. Bring the mixture to a boil, reduce the heat, and simmer, covered, for 15 minutes.

To a saucepan of boiling salted water add the lemon juice and okra. Bring back to a boil, remove from heat, drain the okra, and rinse in cold water. Add the okra to the stock pot with the yams and plantains and cook, covered, over very low heat for 1 hour.

In a skillet, heat the butter and sauté the fish until the fillets are golden. Cut the fish into 1-inch pieces and add to the soup with the tomato paste, Worcestershire sauce, and salt and pepper to taste. Simmer for 10 minutes longer.

Yield: 6 to 8 servings

Heat Scale: Hot

Cuchuco

(Uruguayan Barley Soup)

This soup makes a wonderful light meal; for a heartier dish, add some small cubes of beef to the soup, or use beef shanks. Try serving it with Nicaraguan Jalapeño Pork Salad (p. 46). Add big crusty rolls for the perfect meal.

1	pound beef bones
4	quarts water
1	large onion, chopped
1	bay leaf
2	teaspoons salt
8	peppercorns, crushed

2	fresh ají chiles, seeds and stems removed, minced, or substitute yellow wax hot chiles or jalapeños
2	cups barley, washed
½	pound fresh green peas
½	white cabbage, finely chopped

Place the beef bones, water, onion, bay leaf, salt, peppercorns, and chile in a large pot. Bring to a boil, lower the heat and simmer, covered, for 3 hours. Place the barley in another pot and add water to cover. Bring to a boil and drain the barley. Return the barley to the pot and cover again with water. Bring to a boil, cook 3 minutes, and drain.

    Strain the beef broth into a large pot and add the barley, peas, and cabbage. Bring to a simmer and cook 45 minutes. Taste for seasoning and serve.

Yield: 8 to 10 servings

Heat Scale: Medium

Sopa de Ajo

(Garlic Soup)

A version of garlic soup is found in most Latin American countries, and this one from Ecuador is particularly tasty. Don't be put off by the idea of an entire soup being devoted to such a potent ingredient; garlic soup, when made well, is smooth, mild, and never overpowering.

1	tablespoon olive oil
2	tablespoons butter
10	large cloves garlic, peeled and mashed
½	teaspoon flour
2	ají chiles, seeds and stems removed, minced, or substitute yellow wax hot chiles or jalapeños
1	quart beef or chicken stock, strained
	Salt and freshly ground white or black pepper to taste
4	large eggs, beaten
2	tablespoons finely grated Romano cheese
1	tablespoon chopped fresh parsley

In a heavy pot, melt the oil and butter and sauté the garlic while quickly stirring in the flour. Stir until the garlic begins to brown. Add the remaining ingredients, except for the parsley, and mix well. Bring to a boil, then reduce the heat to medium, and cook, covered, for 15 minutes. If desired, strain the soup. Keep the soup hot. Garnish with the parsley.

Yield: 4 servings

Heat Scale: Medium

Locro de Zapallo

(Pumpkin Soup with Gruyère Cheese and Cumin)

Here is a popular soup from the world's eighth largest country, Argentina. It stretches from the Tropic of Capricorn to Cape Horn, on the southern tip of South America. This soup is traditionally cooked in earthenware; however, a stock pot will do.

½ pound bacon, chopped

2 onions, chopped

4 pounds fresh pumpkin, peeled and cut into small pieces, or 1 can (29 ounces) unseasoned pumpkin puree

3 ají chiles, seeds and stems removed, minced, or substitute yellow wax hot chiles or jalapeños

2 teaspoons cumin seeds, ground

8 to 10 cups chicken stock

1½ cups grated Gruyère cheese

3 tablespoons chopped parsley

In a stock pot, fry the bacon until it is almost crisp. Add the onions and sauté them until they are very soft. Add the pumpkin, chiles, cumin, and stock and cook, uncovered, over medium heat for 15 to 20 minutes, or until the soup reaches a slightly thick consistency. Add the cheese and heat through, but do not boil. Garnish with chopped parsley.

Yield: 6 servings

Heat Scale: Hot

5

Matambre
Meats That Kill the Hunger

In southern Brazil and Argentina, spicy barbecues called *churrascos* are very popular, especially where the large cattle ranches are located. Beef cuts and sausages are marinated in various chile barbecue sauces, skewered on large "swords," and then grilled. Some of the meat is drenched in sauce, wrapped in papaya leaves, and then buried in the hot coals. The meat is tenderized from the papain contained in the leaves. Our recipe for Chorizo Criollo (Chorizo Sausage, p. 126) is one that would be served at a fiery *churrasco*. We have a selection of barbecue sauces in Chapter 2 for use in barbecues.

The Peruvian counterpart to the Argentinian *churrasco* is the *pachamanca*, a huge food fiesta with

---

107

music, dancing, and drinking. Legend has it that the fiesta is Incan in origin. A huge pit is dug, it is lined with stones, and firewood is added. The contemporary meats that are cooked include lamb, veal, kid, and stuffed fowl. Tamales, sweet potatoes, yucas, and fresh cheese are cooked along with the meat. This "oven" is then covered with banana leaves, and the contents cook for several hours.

The Incas ate deer, wild llama, guanaco, and a large rodent called vizcacha; however, the royalty would not consume dogs, ducks, or *cuy* (guinea pig)—the meat sources loved by the peasants when they could obtain them. Even though llamas were eaten, they were much more valuable as pack animals. According to Stuart Hutson, a llama breeder, the llama is the most sure-footed of all pack animals and can carry in excess of twenty-five percent of its body weight. Dried llama meat is called *charqui,* and it can sometimes be found today; however, donkey or mule is used more often.

Other unusual meats are popular in Latin cooking. In eastern Peru, roasted monkey is reputed to be a favorite meat; we have not included a recipe for it. Another spicy recipe we have not included is *choncholis,* which is a Peruvian dish containing cow's or sheep's intestines that are marinated in vinegar, garlic, chiles, cumin, and salt. *Picante tacneno* is also found in Peru; it is horsemeat jerky that is combined with ají chiles, onions, and potatoes for a stew.

We have kept our meat section to those meats that are readily available in the North American markets. Imagine your butcher's surprise if you asked for a three-pound monkey and two pounds of tapir meat!

We include two spicy recipes for Andean stuffed rocoto chiles; Rocotos Rellenos Numero Uno (Stuffed Chiles No. 1, p. 112) uses pork, and the chiles are dipped in egg whites and deep fried. Rocotos Rellenos Numero Dos (Stuffed Chiles No. 2, p. 114) uses beef and raisins and is baked—both recipes are delicious.

Some of the pork recipes can stand on their own as one-dish meals—add a salad and dinner is ready! An example of such a dish is Ají de Carne (Peppery Pork with Bananas, p. 115) containing chiles, spices, potatoes, and bananas. Cerdo Picante (Spiced Pork, p. 116) is crispy cubes served over split peas with spices, and the chile adds a flame of heat. Cara Pulcra (Pork with Dried Potatoes, p. 118) has Incan origins with the use of *papa seca* (dried, ground potatoes) and the spice of ají chiles. The unusual Chicharrones con Camotes (Fried Pork Ribs with Sweet Potatoes, p. 120) is fast, spicy, and delicious. A note to lovers of U.S. Southwest cuisine: the *chicharrones* in this recipe are pork ribs, not the fried pork rinds so beloved by George Bush! Chancho Picante (Spicy Pork with an Asian Touch, p. 122) is a delectible collision of east and west. The spicy chile pork is tempered with the addition of soy sauce and peanuts and is served over rice, a staple in the east as well as in Latin America. Cerdo con Limón (Pork with Lime, p. 123), and Porco Moda Amazonas (Amazon-Style Pork, p. 124) both incorporate citrus juice. Many Latin American cooks believe that citrus enhances the flavor of pork; therefore, you will find many recipes using this combination.

Naturally, beef is a major player in South American cuisine, considering the vast pampas, the incredible number of beef cattle, and those great cookouts—the *churrascos*. One component of the famous *churrascos* is spicy, grilled sausage. We have included Chorizo Criollo (Argentinian Chorizo Sausage, p. 126) that is easy to prepare at home because we eliminated the problematic sausage casings. The two *matambre* (translated: kill the hunger) recipes differ with the marinade and the method of cooking. Matambre Numero Uno (Stuffed and Rolled Flank Steak, p. 127) uses a beer-vinegar marinade and is simmered on top of the stove, while Numero Dos, p. 128, uses only red wine vinegar and is braised in the oven. Take your pick; they are both delicious! The beef of the pampas prevails again with Biftec al Horno (Uruguayan Baked Beef, p. 130) that is simple, spicy, and spectacular.

Moving along to Brazil, we offer Carne Picadinho (Minced Meat, Brazilian-Style, p. 132), which is a recipe that has numerous permutations; a version of it is found in almost every Latin American country, complete with stories and legends. Another Brazilian beef dish is Bifes (Bahian Beef Steaks, p. 134), a food fit for the Bahian gods; the palm oil is traditional in Bahian cooking, and it was brought to Brazil by the African slaves.

From the western side of the continent we offer Pastel de Choclo (Chilean Meat Pie, p. 135), which combines chile and corn in this hot and spicy dish so typical of Chilean cuisine. In Peru, cheese and chiles are combined in a sauce that is usually reserved for potatoes, but the recipe for Lomo a la Huancaina (Steaks with Cheese and Chile Sauce, p. 136) offers a new twist on a traditional favorite.

The first recipe representing Central American cookery is Biftec con Jalapeños Estilo la Junta (La Junta Jalapeño Steaks, p. 138) from Costa Rica. Costa Rican beef steak is excellent, and, in this recipe, the steaks are topped with an unusual cream and jalapeño sauce. In the Guatemalan favorite, Carne en Jocon (Beef in Tomato and Chile Sauce, p. 140), the beef is simmered with chiles and tomatillos and is thickened with softened tortillas. From Panama, we offer Biftec Picante con Tomate al Estilo Panameño (Panamanian Hot Tomato Beef, p. 141), which is highly seasoned with habanero hot sauce and tempered with soy sauce and tomatoes.

Because rabbit is so readily available in American markets, we have included the recipe for Conejo en Mole Picante (Venezuelan Rabbit in Spicy Sauce, p. 142). The rabbit is slowly simmered with herbs, fresh ginger, and hot chiles. Goat is featured in Seco de Chivo (Ecuadorian Braised Goat, p. 143), which is an unusual and tasty dish. If young goat is not available, lamb may be substituted.

All in all, a great selection of *carnes* to kill the hunger.

Time Warp

"Once the Spaniards brought cattle to the Americas, the Indians, accustomed to eating llama heart, needed little prodding to broaden their menu to include beef heart, skewered and grilled like shish kebob in a fiery dish called *anticuchos*. Even while forced to adopt the Catholic religion, the Indians refused to compromise on food; a painting of the Last Supper in Cuzco's cathedral shows Christ and his Apostles dining on guinea pig, Andean cheese and hot peppers—obvious anachronisms." —Mary Dempsey

Rocotos Rellenos Numero Uno

(Stuffed Chiles No. 1)

We thank Na Conce for this unique recipe from her collection of Peruvian fare of the 1950s. The heat factor in this dish can be very high, but the other ingredients will temper it somewhat. Serve it with hot slices of fresh corn and rounds of cooked sweet potatoes.

20 red rocoto chiles, or substitute the largest jalapeños available	1 pound cooked green peas
Water to cover	½ teaspoon salt
1 pound pork, cubed	¼ teaspoon freshly ground black pepper
3 cups water	2 hard-boiled eggs, diced
2 tablespoons vegetable oil	4 eggs, separated
2 onions, chopped	Vegetable oil for frying
2 cloves garlic, minced	
1 cup peanuts, toasted and ground	

Wash the chiles, leave the stems intact, open half way, and carefully remove the seeds. Place the peppers in a large pot, cover with water, and boil the chiles slowly for 3 minutes. Drain the chiles carefully, keeping them intact, and set aside.

Place the pork in a medium saucepan, add the 3 cups of water, and bring to a boil. Lower the heat to a simmer and cook for 1 hour, or until the pork is tender. Drain the mixture and reserve the cooking liquid. Grind the pork using a coarse setting on the grinder and set aside.

Heat the oil in a medium skillet and sauté the onions and the garlic. Add the ground pork, peanuts, peas, salt, pepper, and enough of the reserved pork stock to keep the mixture moist. Mix in the chopped eggs and remove from the heat and let the mixture cool for a few minutes.

Stuff the chiles with this mixture and close as tightly as possible.

Beat the egg whites until they are quite stiff and then fold the well beaten egg yolks into the whites.

Heat the oil, and when it is ready, dip each pepper into the egg mixture and deep fry for 30 to 60 seconds, until the outside is golden brown. Drain on paper towels.

Yield: 20 stuffed chiles

Heat Scale: Hot

Winifred Meets the *Cuy*

"While visiting a family friend's home in Quito, Ecuador, I was served first because I was a woman and the invited guest. They placed a dish before me—there was an animal lying across the rice, served with the head and feet all there. It looked like a dead rat on a bed of rice. It was *cuy* [guinea pig], and, of course, I had to eat it. No comment." —Winifred Galarza

Rocotos Rellenos Numero Dos

(Stuffed Chiles No. 2)

You have to grow your own to find rocoto chiles for this recipe, but any hot chiles, large enough to be stuffed, can be substituted, although they may not have the rocoto's true fiery effect. We recommend using large jalapeños. This recipe is from Mary Dempsey, writing in *Chile Pepper*.

½   pound ground beef

1   onion, diced

1   clove garlic, crushed

⅓   cup raisins

2   hard-boiled eggs, chopped

8   black olives, sliced

4   slices bread, soaked in milk then squeezed and drained

½   cup grated Gouda cheese

12   to 16 rocotos, or substitute large jalapeños or yellow wax hot chiles, stems removed and seeds removed through a hole at the top

In a medium skillet, brown the ground beef with the onion and garlic. Remove from the heat and mix in the raisins, hard-boiled eggs, olives, bread, and cheese.

Stuff the chiles with mixture, stopping the opening with a plug of cheese. Place them in a covered casserole dish and bake in a 350°F oven for 20 minutes.

Yield: 4 servings

Heat Scale: Hot

Ají de Carne

(Peppery Pork with Bananas)

The use of bananas in this pork dish is very typical of Latin American cooking. Bolivians have a reputation for liking spicy foods, and this recipe contains enough chile pepper to satisfy even the most jaded palate. Because this is a rich, one-pot meal, we suggest serving a salad of greens and sliced tomatoes, drizzled with olive oil.

3 to 4 tablespoons olive oil

3 cups chopped onion

3 cloves garlic, minced

2½ pounds boneless pork, cut into ½-inch cubes

3 cups chopped tomatoes

¼ teaspoon saffron

½ teaspoon salt

¼ teaspoon freshly ground black pepper

2 tablespoons ají chile powder, or substitute New Mexican, such as Chimayó

⅛ teaspoon ground cloves

¼ teaspoon ground cinnamon

2 cups chicken stock or beef broth

4 medium potatoes, peeled and quartered

2 green bananas, peeled and quartered

½ cup heavy cream or coconut cream

1 tablespoon molasses

½ cup finely chopped cashews or unsalted peanuts

Heat the oil in a heavy Dutch oven casserole and sauté the onion and garlic until the onion is soft. Add the pork, a little at a time, and brown the cubes. Then, add the tomatoes, saffron, salt, black pepper, chile powder, cloves, cinnamon, and stock. Bring this mixture to a boil and then reduce the heat to a simmer, cover, and cook for 30 minutes.

Add the potatoes and the bananas and simmer for 25 more minutes.

Stir in the cream, molasses, and the nuts and simmer until heated through, taking care that the cream does not boil. Serve immediately.

Yield: 5 to 6 servings

Heat Scale: Hot

Cerdo Picante

(Bolivian Spiced Pork)

This delicious and unusual Bolivian recipe is a great one-dish meal. The crispy pork contrasts nicely with the spicy peas, and the fresh lemon juice over the top is one more way to add a citrus punch to a pork recipe. Serve the dish with one of the potato recipes from Chapter 8 and a fresh green salad or fresh sliced tomatoes.

4   cups water

1½ cups split peas

2   tablespoons chopped parsley

1   onion, peeled, and stuck with 2 whole cloves

1   large carrot, sliced

1   bay leaf

1   clove garlic, mashed

2   celery ribs, cut into several large pieces

½   teaspoon ground or crushed malagueta chile, or substitute piquin or cayenne

½   teaspoon ground cumin

2   tablespoons olive oil

1   teaspoon salt

1½ pounds boneless, lean pork cut into ½-inch cubes

½   teaspoon ground cumin

1   tablespoon lemon zest

1   teaspoon ground cardamom

½   teaspoon ground malagueta chiles, or substitute piquin or cayenne

½   cup fresh lemon juice

Garnishes: Lemon wedges, stuffed olives

Pour the 4 cups of water into a medium, heavy saucepan and add the washed split peas and the parsley, onion, carrot, bay leaf, garlic, celery, chile, and cumin. Bring to a boil, reduce the heat to a simmer, cover, and cook until the peas are done—about 1 hour. Remove the bay leaf and mash the pea mixture a little with a potato masher. Place the mashed peas in a shallow pyrex pan and smooth it out. Keep the peas warm.

    Heat the oil in a large skillet and add the salt. When the oil is hot, add the pork cubes, a handful at a time, and brown completely after each addition. When all of the cubes are browned, add the remaining ingredients, and stir to mix thoroughly. Continue cooking over medium heat for 5 to 7 minutes until the cubes are crisp and there is no pink left inside the cubes. (Cut one in half to check.) Remember to stir during this process so the meat doesn't burn.

Arrange the crisp pork on top of the peas; garnish with the lemon wedges and the stuffed olives.

Yield: 4 to 6 servings

Heat Scale: Hot

Sorta Like a Rodent Pantry, Right?

"On the west coast of South America, wild, olive-colored guinea pigs are still eaten, but most families, even in the cities, keep at least one cage of domestic guinea pigs in the backyard. Commonplace is the removal of about two kitchen floor tiles to make a pen right in the kitchen floor to hold two guinea pigs and dispose of kitchen vegetable trimmings."

—Calvin W. Schwabe

Cara Pulcra

(Pork with Dried Potatoes)

This is a very simple, spicy, and exotic Peruvian pork main dish that probably dates back to ancient Incan times, with the Incan penchant for drying and freeze drying food. *Papa seca* (dried, ground potatoes) is available in Latin American markets. If you cannot find *papa seca,* it is easy to prepare your own. Clean 2 pounds of small potatoes and boil them in their skins until they are done. Peel the potatoes and put them on a raised screen and dry them in the sun, turning often (or use a food dehydrator). When they are thoroughly dry, grind them in a spice mill and store them in a jar to use as needed.

1	pound *papa seca*	½	cup ground peanuts
	Water for soaking	¼	cup grated ají chiles, or substitute yellow wax hot chiles or jalapeños
2	tablespoons olive oil		
2	tablespoons Achiote Oil (see p. 15)	¼	teaspoon cumin
1	cup finely chopped onion	½	teaspoon salt
1	clove garlic, minced	¼	teaspoon freshly ground black pepper
2	pounds boneless pork, cut into ½-inch cubes	1	to 2 cups chicken stock

Roast the *papa seca* in a dry large skillet, taking care not to burn it. Remove the roasted *papa seca* to a large bowl, cover it with water, and refrigerate overnight. Then put the *papa seca* in a colander and drain thoroughly, pressing down on the mixture.

Heat the oils in a large skillet, add the onion and the garlic, and sauté briefly. Add the cubed pork and brown it; then, add the remaining ingredients and the drained *papa seca* and simmer for 45 to 60 minutes, stirring occasionally and adding more stock or water if the mixture seems too thick.

Note: This recipe requires advance preparation.

Yield: 5 to 6 servings

Heat Scale: Hot

Monkey Business

"The harvest was celebrated by dancing and by excesses of wild intoxication. The hut where the natives were assembled displayed during several days a very singular aspect. There was neither table nor bench; but large, roasted monkeys, blackened by smoke, were arranged in regular order against the wall."

—Alexander von Humboldt

"Brazilians do not cook the heads of monkeys as they do of other animals destined for the table, and even sometimes take the meat from the bones after cooking, to remove all cannibalistic suggestions."

—Cora, Rose, and Bob Brown

Chicharrones con Camotes

(Fried Pork Ribs with Sweet Potatoes)

This easy, tasty recipe is from *Creole Cookery* by Na Conce, which was published in Peru in 1951 and is now quite rare. This cookbook is the repository of some classic household recipes that were prepared by the lady of the house or her cook. The recipes are simple and use basic, available ingredients of the area and the time. The word *chicharrón* refers both to fried pork skins and fried ribs.

4 sweet potatoes, scrubbed	1 cup boiling water
2 pounds pork ribs, cut into individual ribs	2 fresh ají chiles, seeds and stems removed, pureed in a blender, or substitute yellow wax hot chiles or jalapeños
¼ teaspoon salt	
¼ teaspoon freshly ground black pepper	
	Juice of 1 lemon
1 cup cold water	1 teaspoon vinegar
1 clove garlic, mashed	Melted butter
1 large onion, thinly sliced	

Place the sweet potatoes in the oven and bake at 350°F until the potatoes are easily pierced with a fork.

Wash the ribs and pat dry. Sprinkle them with the salt and the pepper.

Pour the cold water into a large, heavy skillet, add the ribs and the garlic, and bring the mixture to a slow boil. Boil the ribs slowly until the water is consumed and the ribs start to fry in their own fat. Stir the ribs and make sure they don't burn, and keep frying until they start to crisp up.

Place the onion slices in a colander and pour the hot water over them. Let stand for 5 minutes, then remove the onion slices and place in a ceramic bowl. Add the pureed chile peppers, lemon juice, and the vinegar. Allow the mixture to marinate for 15 minutes.

Push the ribs to one side of the skillet, add the onion slices, and bring the mixture to a quick boil. Serve immediately, accompanied by slices of hot baked sweet potatoes sprinkled with melted butter.

Yield: 4 servings

Heat Scale: Medium

Coming Soon to a Latin Market Near You

"These big tropical American lizards are one of the most delicate and palatable food animals of America. In nearly all parts of the American tropics where these lizards abound, thousands of iguanas are sold in the markets. The flesh is white, tender, and very similar to young chicken in texture and flavor. The eggs of iguanas are also highly esteemed by the natives, as well as by many northerners residing in the tropics."

—A. Hyatt Verrill

Chancho Picante

(Spicy Pork with an Asian Touch)

This Peruvian recipe is from Mary Dempsey, who wrote: "The Spanish conquistadors brought pigs to Peru, and the Indians soon incorporated pork into their cuisine. This pork dish in a hot sauce, spiced with green onion, peanuts, ginger, and soy sauce also shows the influence Asian immigrants have had on local foods." Serve this dish with white rice or one of the spicier rices in Chapter 8.

1½ pounds pork shoulder
2   tablespoons soy sauce
1½ tablespoons cornstarch, dissolved in ¼ cup cold water
2   teaspoons sugar
4   dried ají chile pods, or substitute New Mexican or pasilla, soaked in water

1   tablespoon white vinegar
2   tablespoons grated fresh ginger
3   tablespoons water
¼   cup peanut oil
½   cup chopped peanuts

Cut the pork into thin strips and place in a large bowl. Add 1 tablespoon of the soy sauce, ⅔ of the cornstarch mixture, and 1 teaspoon sugar and stir well to coat the meat. Set aside for 15 minutes.

Remove the stems and seeds from the chiles and puree them in a blender. In a small bowl, combine remaining soy sauce, sugar, and cornstarch, then add the vinegar, ginger, and 3 tablespoons of water.

Combine the pork strips and the pureed chiles in a bowl. Heat a wok to hot, add the peanut oil, and stir-fry the pork until done, about 5 minutes. Remove the pork from the wok. Put the soy-sugar-ginger mixture and peanuts in the wok, stirring well, until hot. (Add water if the mixture thickens too much.) Mix in the meat and serve immediately.

Yield: 4 servings

Heat Scale: Medium

Cerdo con Limón

(Pork with Lime)

We thank Winifred Galarza for giving us this Ecuadorian recipe. We know there are many variations on this dish because pork is frequently cooked with lime juice (sometimes with the addition of orange juice), and, of course, each cook has a favorite recipe. We suggest serving slices of cooked sweet potatoes with this dish, along with a rice or potato dish from Chapter 8.

2 pounds boneless lean pork, cut into 1-inch cubes	½ cup fresh lime juice
2 to 4 tablespoons flour	2 cups chicken stock
¼ cup vegetable oil	2 teaspoons habanero-based hot sauce
1 tablespoon grated fresh ginger	2 tablespoons mayonnaise (optional)
2 onions, sliced	Lemon wedges, chopped parsley (for garnish)
½ cup tomatoes, peeled and chopped	
2 tablespoons chopped parsley	

In a large bowl, sprinkle the cubes of meat with the flour and toss well. Heat the oil in a large, heavy casserole and add the pork and the ginger. Cook over medium heat for 3 minutes, turning the cubes to brown them slightly.

Add the onions, tomatoes, and the parsley and cook for a few minutes until the onions start to soften. Then add the lime juice, stock, and the hot sauce. Bring this mixture to a boil and then reduce the heat and simmer slowly, uncovered, for about an hour, until the pork is tender and the stock is reduced to a gravy, stirring several times to avoid burning. Just before serving, stir in the mayonnaise (if using). Garnish with the lemon wedges and the parsley.

Yield: 4 to 5 servings

Heat Scale: Medium

Porco Moda Amazonas

(Amazon-Style Pork)

The isolated area of the Amazon, Amazonas, yields this updated recipe containing pork and a blending of some common ingredients of the area—coconut milk and the traditional heavy use of herbs and chiles for seasoning. This rich, herb-flavored dish could be served with a salad of hearts of palm, Bibb lettuce, and fresh tomatoes.

Marinade

1   cup dry white wine
½   cup fresh lemon juice
2   cloves garlic, minced
1   teaspoon sugar
½   teaspoon salt
¼   teaspoon freshly ground black pepper
⅓   cup olive oil
1   teaspoon chopped fresh rosemary
1   bay leaf
1   teaspoon crushed, dried malagueta chile or substitute piquin or cayenne
2½ pounds boneless lean pork, cut into ½-inch cubes

Breading

¾   cup ground Brazil nuts
2   cups bread crumbs
2   teaspoons lemon zest

The Pork

1   cup vegetable oil
2   tablespoons olive oil
1   onion, sliced
3   tablespoons cream
3   tablespoons coconut milk
½   teaspoon dried, crushed tarragon
¾   teaspoon dill weed
½   teaspoon crushed, dried malagueta chile, or substitute piquin or cayenne

Combine all of the ingredients for the marinade in a large ceramic bowl or pan. Add the cubed pork and toss the cubes to coat them with the marinade. Cover and refrigerate the pork to marinate for 4 to 6 hours.

Drain the pork in a colander, and reserve the marinade.

Toss the pork cubes in the Brazil nuts, bread crumbs, and lemon zest.

Heat the vegetable oil in a large, heavy skillet, and when it is hot, add the pork cubes, a few at a time, tossing them in the pan to brown, taking care not to burn them. As the pork cubes brown, remove them to paper towels to drain and arrange them on a platter and keep them warm.

Heat the olive oil in a medium skillet, add the onion, and sauté until the onion is soft. Pour in the reserved marinade and bring the mixture to a boil, lower the heat to a simmer, and simmer the mixture for 12 minutes. Add the remaining ingredients and heat through, but do not boil.

Pour the warmed sauce over the heated pork cubes and serve immediately.

Note: This recipe requires advance preparation.

Yield: 6 to 7 servings

Heat Scale: Hot

Chorizo Criollo
(Argentinian Chorizo Sausage)

These delicious sausages have a counterpart all over Latin America. The ingredients can vary widely; some recipes call for saltpeter, some use all pork, some include spices such as cloves and cinnamon, and still others prefer vinegar or wine. We have included this rather traditional recipe from Argentina utilizing the famed ají p-p, the "bad word" chile; for a substitute, use pure hot red chile powder, such as New Mexican Chimayó. In Argentina, these sausages are almost always included at an *asado*—a barbecue.

2	pounds boneless pork	½	teaspoon cumin
1	pound round steak	6	peppercorns, crushed
½	pound fresh bacon (available at natural food markets)	2	teaspoons ají p-p chile powder, or substitute hot red chile powder, such as cayenne or New Mexican Chimayó
½	teaspoon salt		
1	clove garlic		
1½	teaspoons oregano	¾	cup dry white wine

Coarsely grind the pork, round steak, bacon, salt, and garlic together in a meat grinder or food processor. If you use a food processor, take care not to grind the meat too finely; you want the meat to have some texture.

Place the ground meats in a large ceramic bowl, add the remaining ingredients, mix thoroughly, cover, and refrigerate for 24 hours.

Form the meat into 12 to 14 patties and fry them in a skillet over medium heat for 3 to 4 minutes per side, or until no pink remains on the inside. Drain the patties on paper towels and serve hot.

Note 1:   This recipe requires advance preparation.

Note 2:   The uncooked patties freeze well for future use; after forming the patties, layer them between sheets of plastic wrap, then wrap securely for the freezer. That way, you can pull off one or several patties to thaw and fry.

Yield: 12 to 14 patties

Heat Scale: Medium

Matambre Numero Uno
(Stuffed and Rolled Flank Steak)

From the Spanish words *matar,* to kill, and *hambre,* hunger, comes the name for this filling dish. There are many variations on it in Chile and Argentina. It is said to have originated as an easy-to-carry meal on long stagecoach rides across the pampas. This recipe is from *Chile Pepper* food editor Nancy Gerlach. Serve it with any of the potato dishes from Chapter 8.

½ cup beer
½ cup vinegar
¼ cup vegetable oil
2 cloves garlic, minced
1 bay leaf
1 2-pound flank steak
6 fresh ají chiles, seeds and stems removed, chopped, or substitute yellow wax hot chiles or jalapeños

1 cup chopped fresh spinach
2 carrots, peeled and julienned
1 medium onion, thinly sliced and separated into rings
4 slices bacon
1 tablespoon oregano
¼ cup chopped fresh parsley
1 quart beef broth
String for tying

Combine the beer, vinegar, oil, garlic, and bay leaf. Marinate the steak in the mixture for 4 hours.

Remove the steak and flatten it with a rolling pin. Spread the chiles over the meat, then the spinach, carrots, onions, bacon, oregano, and parsley. Roll up the steak, taking care to turn the edges in so the stuffing does not fall out. Tie the roll with string to hold it together.

Place the rolled steak in a pan with the marinade and enough beef broth to come up to the top of the meat. Simmer for 2½ hours or until the meat is very tender.

Note: This recipe requires advance preparation.

Yield: 6 to 8 servings

Heat Scale: Hot

Matambre Numero Dos
(Stuffed and Rolled Flank Steak)

Traditionally, this recipe is thought of as Argentinian; however, it is also popular in Uruguay and other parts of Latin America as well. In the early days, stagecoach travelers would take this meat dish with them for sustenance on the long journeys. The spinach, carrots, and onions seem to be a common denominator in the filling, but some recipes call for variations such as pistachios, raw pork, calves' brains, and peas. It makes a spectacular meat dish for a buffet, and the bonus is that it is prepared ahead of time and can be served hot or cold.

Marinade

2½ pounds flank steak, sliced open horizontally and pounded flat
1   cup red wine vinegar
2   cloves garlic, minced
1   bay leaf
1   teaspoon thyme
1   teaspoon oregano
½   teaspoon cumin
1   tablespoon crushed ají chile powder, or substitute New Mexican

Stuffing

1   small bunch spinach, washed
2   tablespoons chopped parsley
2   ounces salt pork, parboiled and thinly sliced
3   long thin carrots, parboiled
2   cloves garlic, thinly sliced
4   hard-boiled eggs
1   large onion, sliced very thin
1   teaspoon crushed piquin chiles, or substitute cayenne
2   to 3 cups beef stock
    String for tying

Place the steak in a very large, deep roasting pan. Cover with the vinegar, garlic, bay leaf, thyme, oregano, cumin, and chiles. Lift the steak up gently and let some of the mixture flow under the meat. Cover the pan and refrigerate overnight.

Remove the meat from the marinade and allow most of the juice to run off. Spread the meat out flat and cover with the spinach, parsley, and the salt pork. Arrange the carrots across the meat, along with the garlic, eggs, and onion slices and sprinkle with the chile.

Roll the meat tightly, tucking in the ends. Tie the meat every 2 to 3 inches with the string to secure it and to prevent the filling from falling out. Place the tied meat into a heavy casserole or roasting pan and pour in the beef stock. The stock should come half way up the roll; if it doesn't, add some water to make up the difference. Cover and braise in a 350°F oven for 2 to 2½ hours.

To serve hot: Remove the meat roll to a warmed serving plate, let it rest for 15 minutes, remove the string, and cut into 1-inch slices for serving.

To serve cold: Remove the meat to a serving platter, put a plate on top of the meat and put some canned food on top to weigh it down. Refrigerate the meat for several hours or overnight, then remove the string, slice, and serve.

Note: This recipe requires advance preparation.

Yield: 6 to 8 servings

Heat Scale: Medium

Biftec al Horno

(Uruguayan Baked Beef)

Some Latin cooks say that the beef of Uruguay can give some competition to the beef of neighboring Argentina, which only makes sense because the two countries share the plains of the pampas. This simple, easy dish is baked slowly and spiced up with ají chiles. It is a staple menu item in restaurants all over the country, with subtle variations from place to place.

3	tablespoons vegetable oil	¼	teaspoon freshly ground black pepper
4	onions, sliced		
2	cloves garlic, minced	½	teaspoon cayenne powder
1	dried ají chile pod, seeds and stem removed, crushed, or substitute New Mexican	3	tablespoons flour
		2½	pounds round steak
		1	cup beef broth
1	teaspoon salt	2	tomatoes, sliced ¼-inch thick

Heat 1 tablespoon of the oil in a Dutch oven and sauté 1 of the sliced onions, the garlic, and the crushed chile until the onion is soft. Using a slotted spoon, remove the sautéed mixture to a small bowl and set aside.

Mix the salt, black pepper, cayenne, and 2 tablespoons of the flour together and press the mixture into both sides of the round steak. Heat the remaining 2 tablespoons of oil in the casserole and brown the steak on both sides. Cover the steak with the 3 remaining sliced onions and ¼ cup of the broth and cover tightly. Bake in a 350°F oven for 1 hour, or until the meat is tender.

Layer the tomatoes on top of the onions and bake for 15 to 20 minutes more. Remove the meat to a heated platter, allow the meat to sit for a few minutes, and then slice it thinly and keep warm.

Bring the juices in the casserole to a slow boil on top of the stove. Put the remaining 1 tablespoon of flour and the remaining ¾ cup of broth into a jar and shake thoroughly. Slowly strain this mixture into the simmering pan juices and whisk until the mixture is smooth. Add the reserved sautéed onion mixture and heat through. Pour this sauce over the sliced meat and serve immediately.

Yield: 4 to 6 servings

Heat Scale: Medium

Carne Picadinho

(Minced Meat, Brazilian-Style)

This recipe has many permutations as well as names: in Portuguese, it is *carne picadinho;* in Spanish, it is *picadillo;* and in slang, it is called Hangover Hash because it is reputed to be a cure for hangovers. The variations in the recipes are mind-boggling—the simplest recipe we heard about had only seven ingredients, several had twelve to fourteen, and the most ingredients in a recipe of the same name had twenty-five ingredients. We think it depends on the budget and the creativity of the person who is making the dish. Try this version for breakfast with a fried egg on top.

3 tablespoons vegetable oil, more if needed

1 cup finely chopped onion

1 bell pepper, minced

2 cloves garlic, minced

1 pound sirloin, cut into ¼-inch cubes

¼ pound lean pork loin, cut into ¼-inch cubes

¼ pound spicy smoked sausage, such as *chorizo* (see recipe, p. 126), cut into ¼-inch cubes

¼ teaspoon salt

1 habanero chile, seeds and stem removed, minced, or substitute 3 jalapeños

2 tomatoes, peeled, seeded, and chopped

½ teaspoon cumin

½ teaspoon oregano

1 tablespoon red wine vinegar

½ teaspoon sugar

1 cup beef stock

Heat the oil in a large, heavy skillet and sauté the onion, bell pepper, and the garlic until the onion is soft. Push this mixture to one side of the skillet and sauté the sirloin, pork loin, sausage, salt, and the hot peppers, stirring until the meat is slightly browned, and then mix the meat and the onion mixture together.

Add the remaining ingredients and bring the mixture to a boil; reduce the heat to a simmer, cover half of the skillet, and cook for 30 to 45 minutes to blend the flavors and cook off most of the liquid. The mixture will be what is called a "dry" *picadinho.*

Variation 1: Heat 1 cup of additional beef stock to a slow boil. Make a roux of 1 tablespoon butter and 1 tablespoon flour and add it to the hot beef stock and whisk until the mixture is smooth. Add this gravy to the cooking meat and simmer for an additional 15 to 20 minutes, with the skillet covered.

Variation 2: Add cooked, diced potatoes to either the dry or gravy version.

Variation 3: For another "dry" version, top it with chopped, hard-boiled eggs and halved green or ripe olives.

Variation 4: Serve the dried version topped with cooked, diced potatoes and a fried egg.

Yield: 4 to 5 servings

Heat Scale: Medium

Bifes

(Bahian Beef Steaks)

Another food of the Bahian gods (Orixa) are the *bifes* that are actually an English contribution to the great range of Bahian cooking. The English helped the Portuguese to defend Salvador, the capital of Bahia, from pirates. This dish is the food of Exu, who is considered to be the middleman between the gods and the people; the Catholic counterpart is the devil. His colors are red and black, and his element is the streets, according to Tita Libín, who has extensively researched the gods of Bahia. Tita's recipe for *bifes* includes *farofa* (p. 25), which is made from manioc flour and is used extensively in Brazil.

4   thin beef steaks
2   cloves garlic, chopped
1   teaspoon salt
    Freshly ground black pepper
2   to 3 tablespoons palm oil or substitute vegetable oil with 3 teaspoons paprika added
1   small onion, sliced and separated into rings

1   habanero chile, stems and seeds removed, minced, or substitute 3 jalapeños
1   tablespoon lemon juice, fresh preferred
    Farofa (see recipe, p. 25)

Rub the steaks with the garlic and season with salt and pepper.

Heat the oil and pan-fry the steaks until almost done. Add the onions and chile and sauté until the onions are soft. To serve, place the steaks on a plate, sprinkle with the lemon juice, and top with the onion mixture. Sprinkle the *farofa* over the top and serve with rice.

Yield: 4 servings

Heat Scale: Medium

Pastel de Choclo

(Chilean Meat Pie)

This delicious, spicy one-dish meal only needs a large green salad, sliced tomatoes, a potato dish from Chapter 8, and a Chilean wine to create a feast. We have used lean, ground beef in this recipe, but coarsely ground chicken, rabbit, or pork can also be used.

1½ pounds coarsely ground lean beef	½ teaspoon salt
1 to 2 tablespoons vegetable oil	¼ teaspoon freshly ground black pepper
1 cup chopped onion	½ teaspoon oregano
1 large dried ají chile pod, crushed, or substitute New Mexican	10 black olives, cut in half
	2 cups fresh corn
½ teaspoon cumin	1 tablespoon milk
1 teaspoon paprika	1½ teaspoons sugar
	1 tablespoon oil

In a heavy skillet, brown the meat, drain, and put it into a bowl. Add the oil to the skillet, sauté the onion, and add the chile, cumin, paprika, salt, pepper, and oregano; add the sautéed mixture to the meat and mix. Then pack the meat mixture into a shallow 3 to 4 quart ovenproof casserole and arrange the olives over the top.

Put the corn in a blender with the milk, ½ teaspoon of the sugar, and puree the corn. Heat the oil in a skillet, add the pureed corn, and simmer, stirring until the puree thickens. Pour this mixture over the meat mixture and sprinkle with the remaining 1 teaspoon of sugar.

Bake in a 350°F oven for 45 to 60 minutes, or until the top is golden.

Yield: 6 servings

Heat Scale: Mild

Lomo a la Huancaina

(Steaks with Cheese and Chile Sauce)

In Peru, "Huancaina" style usually refers to potatoes sauced with cheese, chile, and onions. In this recipe, there is an interesting twist—the sauce is used over broiled beefsteaks. To complete this dinner, we suggest some baked potatoes and a tomato-cucumber salad drizzled with olive oil and fresh lime juice.

1	small package cream cheese (3 ounces)	¾	cup heavy cream
3	hard-boiled egg yolks	1	tablespoon fresh lemon juice
½	teaspoon salt	¼	cup finely chopped onion
¼	teaspoon freshly ground black pepper	6	steaks
2	teaspoons dried, crushed ají chile, or substitute hot New Mexican	18	ripe olives, halved
		3	hard-boiled eggs, quartered
¼	cup olive oil	6	tablespoons minced Italian parsley

Beat the cream cheese until it is smooth. Press the egg yolks through a sieve into the cream cheese, and add the salt, black pepper, dried chile, and beat into the cheese.

Add the olive oil, a few drops at a time, beating the oil in thoroughly. Add the cream, lemon juice, and the onion and mix in. Pour this mixture into a small saucepan and heat slowly, stirring constantly, and do not allow the mixture to boil. Keep the cheese mixture warm while the steaks are broiling.

Broil the steaks and place them on a heated platter. Top each steak with some of the warm cheese mixture and garnish with the olives, hard-boiled eggs, and parsley.

Yield: 6 servings

Heat Scale: Medium

Vegetarians: Don't Read This Anecdote

"Without pressure from growing population centers, meat was virtually free, left to rot or burned after butchering. In the eighteenth century, people in the cattle zones continued to consume enormous amounts of beef. Cowboys in Argentina ate meat three times a day, washed down with *maté*. Cows were killed daily and their meat hung from the corral posts so hungry workers could cut away what they wanted."

—John C. Super

Biftec con Jalapeños Estilo La Junta

(La Junta Jalapeño Steaks)

This recipe is from Nancy Gerlach, who with her husband Jeff accompanied Dave and Mary Jane to Costa Rica. She wrote: "On the way back to San Jose from the habanero fields in Los Chiles, we stopped at the restaurant La Junta to sample some of the local beef. After enjoying an appetizer of black bean puree, flour tortillas, and cilantro salsa, we were served thick, tender steaks topped with a mild jalapeño sauce."

1 tablespoon olive oil	1 tablespoon coarsely ground black pepper
4 tablespoons butter or margarine	1½ cups beef stock
4 boneless steaks, cut 1-inch thick	⅓ cup heavy cream
¼ cup minced onions	3 jalapeño chiles, stems and seeds removed, cut in thin strips
3 jalapeño chiles, seeds and stems removed, minced	2 tablespoons chopped fresh cilantro
½ cup red wine	

Heat the olive oil and 2 tablespoons of butter in a heavy skillet. Brown the steaks on both sides. Reduce the heat and cook gently until they are medium rare or cooked to desired doneness. Remove from the pan and keep warm.

Pour off the fat. Add the remaining butter to the remaining juices. Add the onion and minced jalapeños and simmer, stirring constantly, until softened.

Add the red wine, bring to a boil, and deglaze the pan, being sure to scrape up any bits that may have stuck to the bottom or sides of the pan. Add the ground black pepper, stock, and cream and bring to a boil. Reduce the heat and simmer until the sauce is smooth and thick.

Place the steaks on a plate, pour the sauce over the top, garnish with the jalapeño slices and cilantro, and serve.

Yield: 4 servings

Heat Scale: Medium

Carne en Jocon
(Beef in Tomato and Chile Sauce)

This spicy beef dish is found throughout Guatemala; it is a famous and traditional favorite that is usually served with hot cooked rice. Mexican green tomatoes, called tomatillos, are available at Latin American markets and even in some chain grocery stores. The tomatillos add an interesting taste dimension with a hint of lemon and herbs.

3 to 4 tablespoons vegetable oil	10 ounces fresh tomatillos, husks removed, and diced; or substitute a 10-ounce can of tomatillos
1 cup chopped onion	
2 cloves garlic, minced	
1 bell pepper, seeded and chopped	3 tomatoes, peeled and chopped
2 fresh serrano chiles, seeds and stems removed, chopped, or substitute jalapeños	1 bay leaf
	¼ teaspoon ground cloves
	1 teaspoon oregano
3 pounds boneless beef, cut into 1-inch cubes	¾ cup beef stock
	2 tortillas
½ teaspoon salt	Water for soaking
¼ teaspoon freshly ground black pepper	

Heat the oil in a heavy casserole and sauté the onion, garlic, and the peppers. Push the mixture to one side of the casserole, and add the beef and brown it lightly. Mix the meat and the sautéed onion, and add the remaining ingredients, except the tortillas and water.

Bring the mixture to a boil, reduce the heat to a simmer, cover, and gently simmer for 2 hours.

Soak the tortillas in cold water for a few minutes. Squeeze the water out and finely crumble the tortillas into the beef. Stir the crumbled tortillas into the beef and simmer for a few minutes until the meat mixture thickens.

Yield: 6 to 7 servings

Heat Scale: Medium

Biftec Picante con Tomate al Estilo Panameño

(Panamanian Hot Tomato Beef)

We thank Alois Dogué for this recipe. Alois is a native Panamanian who certainly knows his way around a kitchen, and he is also the manufacturer of an habanero-based, Panamanian-style hot sauce, which he highly recommends for use in this recipe. Alois recommends serving this dish with hot, cooked rice and some crusty French or Italian bread.

1 pound sirloin steak	2 tablespoons vegetable oil
1 tablespoon soy sauce	2 sliced tomatoes
½ teaspoon seasoning salt	1 large sliced onion
1 teaspoon Habanero Hot! Hot! Hot! Peppersauce Panamanian-Style (or other favorite habanero hot sauce)	¼ teaspoon oregano

Pound the sirloin and then rinse it under running water. Pat the sirloin dry and place it in a large ceramic bowl.

Pour the soy sauce, seasoning salt, and pepper sauce over the steak and marinate for 20 minutes.

In a medium skillet, heat the oil and brown the steak on both sides. Add the tomatoes, onion, and oregano and simmer for 15 minutes.

Yield: Alois says this serves 1 to 2 people; he likes this dish a lot! However, we think this dish will serve 2 to 3, especially with the side dishes.

Heat Scale: Medium

Conejo en Mole Picante

(Venezuelan Rabbit in Spicy Sauce)

Rabbit is readily available in many U.S. markets. It is a mild, tasty white meat—and no, it doesn't taste exactly like chicken! Rabbit is extremely versatile; it can be fried, deep fried, sautéed, and sauced. This spicy sauce can also be used with pork, veal, and poultry.

4 pounds rabbit, washed, dried, and cut into 6 to 8 pieces	1 small green apple, peeled and grated
½ teaspoon salt	½ teaspoon dried tarragon
¼ teaspoon freshly ground black pepper	2 bay leaves
2 teaspoons freshly grated ginger root	1 teaspoon thyme
3 tablespoons vegetable oil	2 tablespoons chopped Italian parsley
1 cup chopped onions	½ cup milk
2 cloves garlic, minced	¾ cup chicken stock
½ teaspoon habanero powder or ¾ teaspoon cayenne	

Season the rabbit with the salt, pepper, and the ginger.

Heat the oil in a large, heavy skillet, add the rabbit pieces, and sauté them until they are browned, turning, about 10 minutes. Remove the rabbit to a heated platter.

Reheat the oil and add the onions and sauté them until they brown. Add the garlic and sauté for 30 seconds. Then add the chile powder, grated apple, tarragon, bay leaves, thyme, and parsley and stir to mix.

Return the browned rabbit to the skillet, add the milk and the stock, cover and simmer for 45 to 60 minutes or until tender. Remove the bay leaves before serving.

Yield: 6 to 8 servings

Heat Scale: Medium

Seco de Chivo

(Ecuadorian Braised Goat)

Winifred Galarza gave us this recipe, which she said is easy to prepare and is quite tender and delicious. It is served with cooked rice. As Winifred reminded us, Ecuadorians, as a rule, don't eat their food as hot as their Peruvian neighbors and will often serve the hot stuff on the side, rather than cooking it into the food.

2   tablespoons olive oil
4   pounds goat or lamb, cut into ¾-inch cubes
1   cup *chicha* or substitute raspberry juice
4   tomatoes, peeled and diced
1   large onion, diced

1   clove garlic, minced
½   teaspoon salt
1   fresh ají chile, seeds and stem removed, chopped, or substitute yellow wax hot chile or jalapeño
Water to cover

Heat the oil in a heavy casserole and brown the meat. Add the remaining ingredients and bring the pot to a boil. Cover the pot and reduce the heat to a simmer and cook for 2 to 3 hours until the meat is tender and the water is consumed. Serve over hot rice.

Yield: 8 servings

Heat Scale: Mild

6

Ají de Gallina
Pungent Poultry

I n this chapter we'll examine the use of poultry in Latin American cuisine. There are many different uses for turkey, chicken, duck, and even the Argentinian ostrich, better known as the rhea.

From Brazil to Peru to Uruguay to Argentina, the chicken and the egg are an intricate part of Latin American cuisine. Poultry is mixed with just about every ingredient one can think of, habanero and garlic in Pollo al Ajo Estilo Peruano (Peruvian Garlic Chicken, p. 146), and cheese, walnuts, and ajís in Ají de Gallina (Piquant Creamed Hen, p. 147). Pollo a la Cazuela (Chicken Casserole, p. 148) combines poultry with root crops such as leeks, as well as rocoto chiles and a variety of spices and vegetables.

In Brazil, much of the cuisine is based on the use of nuts: Brazil nuts, peanuts, almonds, and cashews. This list also extends to pumpkin seeds, such as in Xin-Xin (Spicy Chicken with Pumpkin Seeds, p. 149). Peanuts are one of the best sources of protein readily available to many Latin American countries, and this legume is a main ingredient in Gallina en Salsa de Nueces (Chicken in Nut Sauce, p. 150) from Argentina.

The Mayas raised domesticated turkeys and ducks and probably were the creators of *mole* sauces. They used pumpkin seeds and squash to thicken sauces such as the ones found in Pollo en Salsa de Pipián Rojo (Chicken in Red Pipian Sauce, p. 152). Jocon (Chicken in Green Sauce, p. 154) also has Mayan influences as well as the smoky hot flavor of cobán chiles (or chipotles).

And finally in our nutty chicken category, you'll find Pollo a la Nogal Estilo Peruano (Peruvian Walnut Chicken, p. 155), where the descendants of the Incas' use of chiles is known to be down right hellish!

Pollo Ahumado con Piña (Smoked Pineapple Chicken, p. 156) and Escabeche de Pollo (Bolivian Hot Pickled Chicken, p. 158) are examples of Latin American recipes that combine Old and New World ingredients. Our friend Alois Doqué says that Panamanian cuisine represents the finest combination of Latin American and Caribbean cooking. Check out Doqué's recipe for Pollo con Verduras Estilo Panameño (Panamanian-Style Chicken and Vegetables, p. 160) and decide for yourself.

Along with chicken, duck is a fine ingredient to absorb the heat and flavor of chile peppers. Pato con Arroz Picante (Duck with Spicy Rice, p. 162) offers an extravaganza of tastes and textures intertwining duck, ajís, brandy, and mangoes. Pato Asado com Malaguetas (Orange Chile Duck, p. 163) also features the tropical flavors of nuts and fruits. Pato al Vino Picante (Duckling with Spicy Wine Sauce, p. 164) is exquisitely simple to prepare, but don't let that fool you—this Colombian dish combines the fruity hot taste of the habanero with spices, red wine, and duckling for a heavenly meal. Pato com Môlho de Limão (Duck with Lime Sauce, p. 165) uses Brazil nuts and cognac for a wonderful taste treat.

Even though we have an entire chapter devoted to soups and stews, we've included two wonderful poultry stews in this chapter, Sancoche de Gallina (Peruvian Spiced Chicken Stew with Vegetables, p. 166), and Guisado Maya de Pavo (Mayan Turkey Stew, p. 167), as they so fully and uniquely represent poultry.

And speaking of unique poultry, this book would not be complete without a rhea recipe (p. 168). This Argentinian ostrich is said to have a most wonderful flavor when cooked with chile peppers. Give it a try or substitute turkey for the rhea. Either way, you're guaranteed a great meal.

Pollo al Ajo Estilo Peruano
(Peruvian Garlic Chicken)

Garlic, a member of the onion family, is one of the oldest vegetables used by mankind. There are records of garlic being consumed by the workers who built the pyramids. When the allium was transferred to the New World, it was eagerly added to dishes like this one. Serve this garlic chicken garnished with boiled potatoes, topped with a dollop of yogurt.

½ cup vegetable oil

3 onions, chopped

6 cloves garlic, minced

4 rocoto chiles, seeds and stems removed, minced, or substitute jalapeños

½ teaspoon cinnamon

1 tablespoon cumin seed, crushed

1 teaspoon basil

2 cups peanuts, roasted and coarsely chopped

½ cup freshly grated Parmesan cheese

1 chicken (3½ to 4 pounds) poached, meat removed from the bones, and chopped

¾ cups low-fat plain yogurt, at room temperature

Salt and freshly ground black pepper to taste

Boiled potatoes for garnish

Heat the oil in a large saucepan and sauté the onions and garlic until the onions are soft. Add the chiles, cinnamon, cumin, basil, peanuts, cheese, and the chicken meat to the saucepan and fold together gently. Cook to heat through.

Two or three minutes before serving, stir in the yogurt and correct the seasonings.

Yield: 6 servings

Heat Scale: Hot

Ají de Gallina
(Piquant Creamed Hen)

From Mary Dempsey, writing in *Chile Pepper* magazine, comes another version of Peruvian chicken in a cheese sauce spiced with hot ají chiles. It is served over sliced boiled potatoes and garnished with hard-boiled eggs.

1 carrot, peeled and sliced	¼ cup cooking oil
2 onions; one sliced, one minced	3 cups chicken broth (from reserved broth)
1 4-pound chicken, quartered	1 cup grated Parmesan cheese
½ loaf white bread, crust removed	¼ cup chopped walnuts
1 12-ounce can evaporated milk	6 to 8 potatoes, boiled in their skins until tender, peeled and sliced
8 fresh ají chiles, seeds and stems removed, pureed in a blender, or substitute yellow wax hot chiles or red jalapeños	3 hard-boiled eggs
2 cloves garlic, minced	Freshly ground black pepper to taste

Bring 1 quart of salted water to a boil in a large pot, then add the carrot, sliced onion, and chicken. When the chicken is poached (about 45 minutes), remove it from the water, cool, and shred it into small strips. Strain the broth and reserve the carrot and onion and 3 cups of the broth.

Break the bread into pieces and soak them in the milk. In a large pot, sauté the minced onion, pureed chiles, and garlic in the oil for a few minutes, then add the reserved broth, soggy bread, chicken, cheese, walnuts, and the reserved carrot and onion. Add pepper to taste. Stir over medium heat for about 20 minutes until thick. Place the potatoes on serving plates and pour the chicken sauce over them. Garnish with the hard-boiled egg halves.

Yield: 6 servings

Heat Scale: Hot

Pollo a la Cazuela

(Chicken Casserole)

This chicken recipe features *Capsicum pubescens,* the hairy-leafed chile pepper, better known as the rocoto. Rocotos are typically apple shaped and are said to be hot enough to wake the dead! Substitute jalapeños, as they have a similar thick wall.

1 small chicken	½ cup fresh string beans (cut thinly)
1 tomato, chopped	½ cup fresh peas
1 onion, chopped	½ cup diced celery
1 teaspoon basil	½ cup shredded cabbage
1 teaspoon marjoram	2 bay leaves
½ teaspoon oregano	½ teaspoon freshly ground black pepper
10 cups water	2 rocoto chiles, seeds and stems removed, grated, or substitute jalapeños
1 cup vegetable oil	
1 clove garlic	
½ cup chopped onions	Salt to taste
½ cup diced carrots	Sliced oranges for garnish
½ cup diced leeks	

Cut the chicken into small pieces. In a large pan, place the gizzard, legs, and the carcass of the chicken and add the tomato, onion, basil, marjoram, oregano, and the water, and boil gently for about ½ hour. Dry the chicken pieces; reserve the stock.

Heat the oil in a skillet, and when it is hot, fry the garlic and onion (remove the garlic when brown), add the pieces of chicken and brown, then add the remaining ingredients and cook gently for about 10 minutes. Strain the stock and add 2 cups of it to the stew, and simmer until the vegetables and chicken are done, about 15 minutes. Serve very hot with sliced oranges in each soup bowl.

Yield: 10 to 12 servings

Heat Scale: Medium

Xin-Xin

(Spicy Chicken with Pumpkin Seeds)

This Afro-Brazilian recipe has roots deep in the voodoo religion and is known to be served at black magic rituals. The use of ground prawns and malaguetas reflects its African roots. Serve the *xin-xin* with any of the rices in Chapter 8.

1	3-pound chicken, cut into serving pieces
3	cups water
¼	cup dried, ground prawns or shrimp
½	cup chopped fresh pineapple
¼	cup grated coconut
1½	teaspoons salt
½	cup chopped parsley

2	onions, sliced
1	teaspoon dried crushed malagueta chile, or substitute piquin or cayenne
¾	cup pumpkin seeds, shelled and roasted
1	teaspoon ground coriander
¼	cup vegetable oil
	Parsley for garnish

Place the chicken in a large pan with the water, ground prawns, pineapple, coconut, salt, parsley, onions, and chile. Cover and braise until the chicken is tender (about 30 minutes). Remove the lid and cook until the liquid is reduced by half.

Set aside 10 whole pumpkin seeds for garnish. Grind the rest of the seeds in a spice mill. Add the ground pumpkin seeds to the chicken, together with the coriander and oil. Heat through and serve garnished with parsley and the whole pumpkin seeds.

Yield: 4 to 6 servings

Heat Scale: Hot

Gallina en Salsa de Nueces

(Chicken in Nut Sauce)

Peanuts play a large role in the foods of Latin America. They are a hardy legume that provide both an excellent source of protein and a cooking oil. This easy Argentine recipe pairs peanuts and chiles, a common theme in the region.

1 large chicken, cut up, fat removed	1 cup ground peanuts
4 cups water	2 malagueta chiles, crushed, or substitute piquin or Japanese
1 teaspoon salt	
2 tablespoons butter	2 pimientos, seeds and stems removed, cut julienne, or substitute red bell peppers
½ cup chopped onions	
1 tablespoon cornstarch	
2 tablespoons water	2 tablespoons minced parsley

Combine the chicken and water in a saucepan and bring to a boil; add the salt, cover, reduce the heat, and simmer for 30 minutes. Remove the chicken, drain on paper towels, and keep warm. Continue cooking the broth until it is reduced to 2 cups. Strain and reserve.

Melt the butter in a skillet. Add the onions and sauté until browned, about 10 minutes. Add the reserved broth and heat. Mix the cornstarch with 2 tablespoons cold water and stir it into the broth until thickened. Mix in the peanuts, chile, pimientos, and parsley. Cook, uncovered, over low heat for 5 minutes. Taste for seasoning. Arrange the chicken on a platter and pour the sauce over it.

Yield: 6 to 8 servings

Heat Scale: Medium

Feeding the Inca Royalty

"The food of the imperial family was much more plentiful and varied than that of the common people. The
nobility added fruits from the tropical valleys to this diet,
and above all, in contrast to the common people, they
ate meat—llamas of less than three years of age and
vicuñas less than two years old. The Emperor and his
family were able to make considerable additions to their
diet. These were brought from the different provinces
with great speed by runners; excellent wild duck and
partridges from the *puna* [desert], mushrooms, frogs
from Lake Chinchaychocha, snails, fish and shell-fish
from the Pacific. The whole Empire contributed to the
feeding of the sovereign." —Louis Baudin

Pollo en Salsa de Pipián Rojo

(Chicken in Red Pipian Sauce)

The squash seeds make this a very New World dish, as squash has been a staple of the Central American diet since it was domesticated millennia ago. To add an elegant touch to the end of this Guatemalan meal with Mayan origins, you might serve your guests Champurrado, or Guatemalan Chocolate Coffee (p. 252).

1	chicken, about 3½ pounds, cut into serving pieces, loose skin and fat discarded
4	cups water
1	teaspoon salt, or to taste
1½	cups ripe tomatoes, chopped
½	cup tomatillos, chopped
1	pasilla chile, seeds and stem removed
1	guajillo chile, seeds and stem removed, or substitute New Mexican
¼	cup lime juice
½	cup sesame seeds

1	tablespoon squash seeds (*pepitas*)
1	cinnamon stick, 1-inch long, broken up
2	teaspoons crushed hot New Mexican red chile
½	cup French bread, cubed and moistened with broth
¼	teaspoon achiote (annatto seed)
1	tablespoon flour
	Toasted squash and sesame seeds for garnish

In a skillet, cook the chicken in 3 cups of the water and the salt over medium heat for 30 minutes. Remove the chicken, keep warm, and reserve the broth for the sauce.

Combine the tomatoes, tomatillos, and chiles in ¾ cup water and ¼ cup lime juice and cook over medium heat for 10 minutes.

Toast the sesame seeds, squash seeds, cinnamon stick, and crushed chile in a dry skillet over low heat for about 10 minutes.

In a food processor or blender, process the toasted ingredients, and then add the cooked tomato mixture, stirring into a smooth paste. Add the bread, achiote, 2 cups of chicken broth, and flour and process everything until smooth. Return the sauce to the stove and heat through.

Place the cooked chicken on a platter and cover with the red sauce. Sprinkle the squash and sesame seeds over the top. Serve with Coconut-Chile Rice (p. 213).

Yield: 4 servings

Heat Scale: Medium

You Could Probably Get Andes Oysters, Too

"Regardless of your travel disposition, probably the best deal of all is dining in this country [Ecuador]. I found that most establishments offer what's called *almuerzo* (lunch) or *cena* (dinner) that are all inclusive meals for a set price. A place I frequented in Quito offered a different *almuerzo* every day for $.70 and included fresh juice, soup, bread, meat, vegetable, and coffee. I have eaten in both the common local restaurants and in some of the best restaurants in the larger cities, and even in the most expensive restaurants where the food and atmosphere are excellent, the bill was a fraction of what one would pay in the States. Check what you're ordering though. Once I ended up with a large piece of chicken-fried cow udder *(ubre fritada)*, because I didn't bother to look up *ubre* in my pocket dictionary."

—David Parrish

Jocon

(Chicken in Green Sauce with Smoked Chiles)

This Mayan dish was originally made with turkey or duck. After the Spanish introduced chickens, onions, and cilantro to Guatemala, this recipe evolved. Cobán chiles are used in this dish, but since they are difficult to find outside of Guatemala, another smoked chile—the chipotle—is substituted. Serve the *jocon* with black beans, corn tortillas, and sliced mango.

1 3-pound chicken, cut into serving pieces	1 tablespoon pumpkin seeds
1 onion, chopped	½ cup chopped fresh cilantro
2 cloves garlic, chopped	1 cup sliced scallions, including the greens
1 quart water	½ cup canned tomatillos, drained and chopped
4 dried cobán chiles, stems removed, or substitute 2 dried chipotle chiles	1 tablespoon vegetable oil

Cover the chicken, onion, and garlic with water, bring to a boil, reduce the heat, and simmer until done, about 30 minutes, skimming off any foam that forms. Remove the chicken, strain and reserve the broth.

Cover the chiles with boiling water and allow them to sit for 15 minutes to soften.

Toast the pumpkin seeds in a hot skillet until they start to brown, taking care not to let them burn. Grind the seeds in a blender or spice mill.

Combine the chile, toasted seeds, cilantro, scallions, and tomatillos in a blender along with 2 cups of the chicken broth and puree until smooth.

Remove the skin and brown the chicken in the oil.

Combine the sauce with 1 cup of the reserved broth and pour it over the chicken. Simmer for 15 minutes before serving.

Yield: 4 servings

Heat Scale: Hot

Pollo a la Nogal Estilo Peruano
(Peruvian Walnut Chicken)

Here is another chicken and nut recipe, with walnuts being the favored nut this time. Walnuts were introduced by the Spanish, and today are popular throughout Latin America. A great accompaniment to this recipe is the Jicama and Orange Salad (p. 38) and a salsa from Chapter 2.

3 chickens, cut up	1 teaspoon cumin
Water to cover	½ teaspoon coriander
1 loaf bread, crust removed	Freshly ground black pepper to taste
1 can evaporated milk	
2 tablespoons ají chile powder, or substitute New Mexican	1 cup grated Parmesan cheese
	½ cup walnuts, peeled and finely ground
1 onion, minced	
½ cup vegetable oil	4 hard-boiled eggs, sliced
1 teaspoon salt	

Cook the chickens in boiling water until tender, about 25 minutes. Shred the chicken and set aside.

Soak the crustless bread in the milk in a separate container. Add the chile powder and mix.

Place the onion in a skillet with the oil and sauté. When the oil comes to a boil, add the salt, cumin, coriander, and pepper to taste. Cook the mixture for a while, then add the soaked bread, mashed smooth. Next add the shredded chicken and the grated cheese. Simmer for 20 minutes, covered, checking to see that the mixture does not burn. Then add the walnuts, stirring to blend them in. Serve hot, garnished with hard-boiled eggs.

Yield: 12 to 14 servings

Heat Scale: Medium

Pollo Ahumado con Piña
(Smoked Pineapple Chicken)

The pineapple plant, or *Ananas comosus,* is a native of Central America, and pineapples were first discovered by Christopher Columbus on his second voyage to the West Indies. This Guatemalan recipe combines the delicious fruit with chicken and smoked chiles.

1	medium sized chicken, cut up	3	carrots, sliced
3	cups water	½	pound sugar snap peas or snow peas
	Salt and freshly ground black pepper	1	cup chopped fresh pineapple
1	onion, chopped	2	teaspoons oregano
3	tablespoons vegetable oil	½	teaspoon turmeric or saffron
2	teaspoons finely chopped parsley	½	teaspoon salt
1	red bell pepper, seeded and finely sliced	½	teaspoon freshly ground black pepper
1	green bell pepper, chopped	½	teaspoon cumin
3	cobán chiles, or substitute 2 chipotles, soaked in water and then pureed	1½	cups canned tomatoes with liquid
2	cloves garlic, minced	2	cups rice
		3	cups chicken broth
		¼	cup raisins

In a large pot, combine the chicken with 3 cups of water and the salt and pepper to taste and cook until tender, about 25 minutes. Remove the chicken, reserving the broth, and cut into bite size pieces.

In a large pot, sauté the onion in the oil with the parsley until clear, but not brown. Add the bell peppers, smoked chiles, garlic, carrots, peas, pineapple, oregano, turmeric, salt, pepper, and cumin, stirring over low heat. Simmer for 5 minutes. Add the tomatoes with liquid, rice, reserved chicken, broth, and raisins; mix well. Bring to a boil. Reduce heat, cover, and simmer for 20 to 25 minutes until the liquid is absorbed.

Yield: 4 to 5 servings

Heat Scale: Medium

The Ají Monolith

About A.D. 900, a sculptor of the Chavín culture in Peru carved elaborate designs into a sharp-pointed granite shaft measuring eight feet long and a foot wide, which has become known as the Tello Obelisk. The principal figure on this obelisk is a mythical creature, the black caiman. The sharp point of the stone corresponds to a real caiman's narrow snout, and the end of the stone is carved with the feet and claws of the reptile, which are holding the leaves and pods of a chile plant. As yet, no scholar has deciphered the meaning of a magical caiman grasping chile peppers in its claws, but the image is suggestive of the magical powers that the people of the Andes believed were inherent in the powerful pods.

Escabeche de Pollo

(Bolivian Hot Pickled Chicken)

Most Latin Americans know that *escabeche de pescado* (fish) is often wickedly hot. Here's fair warning that the chicken equivalent of this recipe also offers a suitable amount of heat through the use of habaneros. Serve this in large soup bowls accompanied with warm corn tortillas.

1 large chicken, cut into pieces	½ cup olive oil
2 large onions, thinly sliced	1 cup red wine vinegar
2 fresh habaneros, seeds and stems removed, minced, or substitute 6 jalapeños	1 large bay leaf, crumbled
3 carrots, peeled and cut into quarters	¼ teaspoon ground nutmeg
	Salt and pepper to taste
1 red bell pepper, seeded and sliced	

Combine all ingredients in a pot and cook, covered, over low heat for about 40 minutes. Skim off any foam that forms. Correct the seasoning and let it cool before serving.

Yield: 4 servings

Heat Scale: Hot

What Not to Eat in Brazil

"On our first day in Belem we ate *pato no tucupi,* a regional favorite consisting of duck and greens that seemed marinated in novocaine, for it numbs the mouth. *Tucupi* is prepared from the soft white pulp of the manioc root, in which, according to legend, the beautiful daughter of an Indian chief was hidden after her death. But that starchy root alone cannot explain the effects of the dish. Our mouths were rendered senseless from it; the after-meal coffee trickled out of the side of London's mouth, so incapable was he of controlling the deadened muscles." —Brian Kelly and Mark London

Pollo con Verduras Estilo Panameño

(Panamanian-Style Chicken and Vegetables)

We thank Alois Dogué for this wonderful recipe that incorporates the peppery, hot flavor of Latin America. Alois told us that much of the food of Panama (his home) uses the best of Latin America as well as the best of the Caribbean. He would like the cook to use his Habanero Hot! Hot! Hot! Panamanian-Style Pepper Sauce for this dish, as it is a family recipe. However, feel free to use any bottled habanero sauce.

1	3-pound chicken, cut into 6 pieces	2	green bell peppers, seeded and cut into medium pieces
1	teaspoon salt	⅛	cup Habanero Hot! Hot! Hot! Pepper Sauce or substitute other bottled habanero sauce
1	teaspoon oregano		
¼	cup vegetable oil	2	carrots, sliced
2	teaspoons achiote powder	1	chayote squash, peeled and diced (or substitute zucchini)
1	cup water		
3	tablespoons tomato paste	1	potato, peeled and diced
1	medium onion, chopped	1	12-ounce can kidney beans, drained
1	medium tomato, coarsely chopped		
1	teaspoon chopped cilantro		

Wash the chicken pieces and pat them dry. Season the chicken with the salt and ½ teaspoon of the oregano.

Heat the oil in a large, heavy skillet. Add the achiote powder to the oil and simmer for 3 minutes.

Add the chicken to the oil and sauté until it is golden brown. Add the water, tomato paste, onion, fresh tomato, cilantro, green peppers, and the remaining ½ teaspoon of oregano, and cover and simmer for 25 minutes.

Add the pepper sauce and all of the vegetables and beans and simmer until the vegetables are tender, about 15 to 20 minutes. Serve over hot, cooked white rice.

Yield: 4 to 5 servings

Heat Scale: Hot

Amazon River Dining

"In contrast to the elaborate fish preparations of Belem, meals in most river towns—and on the boat—tended to be boiled fish served with a bowl of pebbly farina. The blandness was overcome by chopped hot peppers potent enough to make an unsuspecting gringo gasp. Chicken, which we gathered must be considered a treat by the approving nods it won when served the first day on the boat, bore little resemblance to the supermarket variety. These birds had legs so sinewy and chests so meager that we reasoned they had been herded to market over a long hard road."

—Brian Kelly and Mark London

Pato con Arroz Picante

(Duck with Spicy Rice)

The Incas were said to have kept domesticated ducks as well as jungle fowl. This Peruvian duck dish combines citrus and the hot ají chile to create a flavorful entree.

2	tablespoons vegetable oil	1	tablespoon ají chile powder, or substitute New Mexican
1	duck, cut up	5	cups water
1	large onion, chopped	2½	cups rice, washed
1½	cups chopped tomatoes	1½	cups fresh green peas
2	cloves garlic, minced	4	tablespoons brandy
	Salt to taste	1	mango, peeled, seeded, pureed
1	tablespoon finely chopped parsley		

Heat the oil in a saucepan, add the pieces of duck, and fry them to a golden brown. Add the chopped onion, tomatoes, garlic, salt, parsley, and chile powder. Sauté for a minute, stirring well. Add 5 cups of water and stew until tender, about 20 minutes. Next, add the rice and peas, cover, reduce the heat, and cook for about 25 minutes. When the rice is cooked, stir in the brandy and the pureed mango.

Yield: 4 servings

Heat Scale: Medium

Pato Asado com Malaguetas

(Orange Chile Duck)

The Portuguese navigator Pedro Cabral was the first European to visit Brazil in 1500, and he didn't have to bring ducks with him. This dish is both hot and sweet at the same time, which makes it reminiscent of Chinese dishes. Serve this with any of the bean dishes in Chapter 8.

1 4-pound duck	½ cup dry white wine
¼ cup orange juice	1 teaspoon malagueta chile powder, or substitute cayenne
¼ cup pineapple juice	
Salt to taste	1 tablespoon vegetable oil
Freshly ground black pepper	2 tablespoons blackberry jelly
Strip of lime peel	2 tablespoons raisins
1 onion, chopped	10 whole jalapeño chiles for garnish
1 scallion, chopped	
1 clove garlic, crushed	2 oranges, sliced in thin rounds

Split the duck in half and place it in a shallow glass bowl. Mix together the orange juice, pineapple juice, salt, pepper, lime peel, onion, scallion, garlic, wine, and chile. Pour the sauce over the duck and marinate in the refrigerator for 1 to 3 hours, turning occasionally. Remove the duck and place it skin-up in a roasting pan. Brush with the oil and bake in a 350°F oven for 1 hour, basting with the reserved marinade mixed with the blackberry jelly.

When the duck is cooked, transfer to a heated platter. Pour off any fat, and add the raisins to the pan drippings, together with any remaining marinade. Bring to a boil on top of the stove and cook for a few minutes, scraping the bottom of the pan as the mixture cooks. If you do not have enough liquid, add stock or water. Pour the sauce around the duck and garnish with the jalapeños and orange slices.

Yield: 4 servings

Heat Scale: Medium

Pato al Vino Picante

(Duckling with Spicy Wine Sauce)

The secret to this succulent dish is the combination of wine and fruity habaneros—they flavor the duck to perfection. The heavy use of peppers and spices in this recipe is highly representative of the evolution of Spanish cuisine into Colombian cuisine.

1	4½- to 5-pound duckling	1	1-inch piece of cinnamon stick
	Salt, freshly ground black pepper	2	teaspoons cardamom
2	tablespoons butter	1	whole habanero chile, or substitute 3 jalapeños
2	large onions, finely chopped	1	cup dry red wine
1	bay leaf	1	cup chicken stock
2	whole cloves		

Preheat the oven to 350°F. Pull the loose fat from inside the duckling and prick the bird all over with a fork to help release excess fat. Season inside and out with salt and pepper. Heat the butter in a heavy casserole and sauté the duckling until it is golden brown all over. Lift out and set aside.

Spoon off all but 4 tablespoons fat from the casserole. Add the onions and sauté until soft. Return the duckling to the casserole. Tie the bay leaf, cloves, cinnamon, cardamom, and habanero in a square of cheesecloth and add to the casserole with the red wine and chicken stock. Season to taste with more salt and pepper if necessary, and bring to a boil on top of the stove. Cover with aluminum foil, then the casserole lid, and bake in a 250°F oven for 1½ hours, or until the duckling is tender.

Lift out onto a serving platter and keep warm. Remove and discard the cheesecloth bag. Skim excess fat from the sauce. If there seems to be an excessive amount of sauce, place the casserole over high heat quickly to reduce it. Spoon a little sauce over the duckling and serve the rest separately. Serve with rice with coconut and raisins and a green salad.

Yield: 4 servings

Heat Scale: Medium

Pato com Môlho de Limão

(Duck with Lime Sauce)

No Latin American cookbook would be complete without a Brazilian recipe calling for limes and Brazil nuts. The nuts make this dish a delicious entree. It may appear that the duck is overcooked, but trust us on this one. Try serving it with our Onion Chile-Cheese Appetizer (p. 41) for a spicy good start.

1   4-pound duck
2   cups lime juice
2   cups orange juice
1   bay leaf
2   teaspoons salt
½   teaspoon freshly ground black pepper

2   habanero chiles, seeds and stems removed, minced, or substitute 6 jalapeños
¼   cup cognac
3   bananas, cut in 2-inch pieces
1   tablespoon cornstarch
¼   cup slivered Brazil nuts
¼   cup Cointreau

Wash and dry the duck; bring the citrus juices and the bay leaf to a boil in a large pot. Add the duck and cook, covered, over low heat for 1 hour, turning the duck several times. Drain, skim the fat, and reserve 3 cups of the citrus stock. Season the duck with the salt and pepper and minced chiles. Place it in a shallow roasting pan. Roast in a 450°F oven for 20 minutes. Add the remaining citrus stock, the cognac, and the bananas. Reduce heat to 350°F and roast 30 minutes longer, basting frequently. Transfer the duck and bananas to a serving platter and keep warm.

Skim the fat from the pan gravy, and pour the gravy and reserved stock into a saucepan. Mix the cornstarch with a little water to make a smooth paste; stir into the gravy until thickened. Add the Brazil nuts and Cointreau; cook over low heat for 5 minutes.

Carve the duck, place on a serving platter, and pour some sauce over it.

Yield: 4 servings

Heat Scale: Hot

Sancoche de Gallina

(Peruvian Spiced Chicken Stew with Vegetables)

The combination of poultry and the sweet potatoes in this dish gives it an extraordinary taste. This soup is hearty enough to work as a main meal, but feel free to accompany it with any of the dishes in Chapter 8.

8	cups water	8	sprigs celery leaves
2	teaspoons salt	3	potatoes, peeled and cubed
1	2- to 3-pound chicken, cut into serving pieces	2	sweet potatoes, peeled and cubed
1	pound beef marrow bones	½	cup corn kernels
2	onions, sliced into rings	1	green bell pepper, seeded and cubed
2	rocoto chiles, seeds and stems removed, chopped, or substitute jalapeños	¾	pound pumpkin, seeded, peeled, and cubed
2	leeks, sliced into rings		Freshly ground black pepper

Bring the water and salt to a boil in a large saucepan. Add the chicken and beef bones. Lower the heat, cover, and simmer for 2 hours. Strain the broth into a clean saucepan. Discard the skin and bones from the chicken and the beef bones. Cut the chicken meat into small pieces and reserve.

Add the remaining ingredients to the broth, cover, and simmer for 30 minutes. Add the chicken meat and simmer 5 minutes more. Taste for seasoning and serve.

Yield: 6 servings

Heat Scale: Medium

Guisado Maya de Pavo

(Mayan Turkey Stew)

The turkey was the Mayan god of rain and fertility and was called *tlaloc*. A meal to the Mayans consisted of a stew, either with meat and vegetables or vegetables alone in a broth base. This stew also uses mint, or native *yerba buena,* as well as cilantro for flavoring. Serve with an avocado salad and corn tortillas.

4	pasilla chiles, seeds and stems removed, or substitute New Mexican	¼	cup chopped cilantro
		¼	cup chopped *yerba buena* or mint
4	jalapeño chiles, stems and seeds removed, chopped	1	small turkey, cut into serving pieces, or substitute duck (be sure to remove the fat if duck is used)
3	tomatoes, peeled		
1	onion, chopped		
1	teaspoon achiote	4	cups water, or more if needed

Cover the pasilla chiles with hot water and let them sit for 15 minutes until softened.

Combine the chiles, tomatoes, onion, achiote, and the water in which the chiles were soaking in a blender and puree until smooth. Stir the cilantro and mint into the sauce.

Place the turkey pieces and water in a pan. Add the sauce, bring to a boil, reduce the heat, cover, and simmer until the turkey is tender, about 1 hour.

Yield: 6 to 8 servings

Heat Scale: Medium

Rhea en Nido

(Rhea on the Nest)

The rhea, or Argentine ostrich, is a smaller cousin of the Australian ostrich. Rheas are widely available in Argentina and are often hunted with *bolas,* braided lariats with lead-filled rawhide balls that wrap around the legs of the bird. If you can't find rhea meat at your local supermarket, turkey will work as a substitute. However, it should be noted that some mail order game companies carry ostrich meat. Serve this with one of the bean dishes from Chapter 8.

6	thin steaks cut from the thigh of the rhea, or substitute slices from the leg or breast of turkey	¼	teaspoon grated nutmeg
		1	whole clove
		1	bay leaf
1	cup salted water	¼	cup olive oil
2	tablespoons vinegar	1	red onion, cut into rings
4	cloves garlic, mashed	1	red bell pepper, chopped
3	ají chiles, seeds and stems removed, minced, or substitute yellow wax hot chiles or jalapeños	1	green bell pepper, chopped
		6	mushrooms, chopped
		3	cloves garlic, minced
			Olive oil
1	cup minced red bell pepper		Freshly ground black pepper
2	teaspoons Louisiana-style hot sauce	6	fresh cabbage leaves
¼	teaspoon marjoram		

Wash the steaks in the salt water, shake off excess water, and set aside. In a large bowl, combine the vinegar, garlic, chiles, bell pepper, hot sauce, marjoram, nutmeg, clove, and bay leaf. Place the steaks in the marinade and let sit in the refrigerator for 1 hour, turning the steaks often.

In a deep casserole pan, heat the olive oil. In a bowl, combine the onion, bell peppers, mushrooms, and garlic and place in the casserole in the shape of six nests. Remove the steaks from the marinade. Roll up each steak and place it in the center of the vegetable nests. Sprinkle with olive oil and freshly ground black pepper. Cover each steak with cabbage leaves and press down. Cover the casserole and cook over low heat for 1 hour.

Yield: 6 servings

Heat Scale: Medium

7

Frutas del Mar
Exotic Fruits of the Sea

The incredibly long coastline of Latin America yields a wide variety of fish and shellfish. There is tremendous diversity, and some of the varieties seldom find their way to the North American markets. For example, the *congrio* (a type of conger eel), one of the most popular fish in Chile, is not available, so we have not included any recipes for it.

We did include a large collection of seven authentic ceviche (or seviche) recipes, the majority of which are from Peru, Ecuador, and Chile. The raw fish or shellfish is marinated in lime and/or lemon juice, and the juices "cook" the fish, so that no additional cooking is necessary.

Such seafood delights are usually considered appetizers in South America; however, given the American propensity for healthy, light entrees (especially for lunch), we suggest that any one of the ceviche

recipes be served as a spicy entree, complete with all of the interesting accompaniments. In Peru ceviche is served with cooked sweet potatoes, lettuce, rounds of cooked corn, and *cancha* (toasted corn). Ceviche de Corvina (Peruvian Sea Bass Ceviche, p. 174) calls for sea bass, which is reputed to be the most delicate tasting fish used in ceviches. Sometimes a mixture of seafood is used, as in Ceviche Mixto de Mariscos Peruano (Peruvian Mixed Seafood Ceviche, p. 176), which utilizes fish, clams, oysters, and mussels. Ceviche de Camarones (Ecuadorian Marinated Shrimp, p. 178) is the fastest to prepare if you use precooked tiny shrimp. The bitter orange used in Ceviche con Naranja Agria (Ceviche with Bitter Orange, p. 179) is actually a Seville orange that is used in Peru and Ecuador. Ceviche de Huachinango Marinado Estilo Peruano (Marinated Snapper Peruvian-Style, p. 180) uses citrus juice as well as vinegar, while fresh hot peppers and hot sauce jazz up Pescado Marinado Estilo Chileno (Marinated Halibut Chilean-Style, p. 181). Ceviche de Ostras (Guatemalan Marinated Oysters, p. 182) sizzles with the habanero chiles and cools down with the addition of mint. The two *escabeche* recipes (p. 183 and p. 184) are an unusual way to serve fish. *Escabeche* seems to be of Arab (Moorish) origin, as a very early method of preserving food and was brought to Latin America by the early Spanish.

Seldom does food play a major role in the literary world, but the foods of Salvador in Bahia, Brazil, have a starring role in many of Jorge Amado's novels. The four Bahian recipes featured here are representative of that special area of Brazil that has been so influenced by the cooking of the African slaves. Eja (Bahian Snapper with Malagueta Shrimp Sauce, p. 186) is a snapper dish that includes dried shrimp, which is frequently used in Bahian cuisine. Bobó de Camarão (Bahian Spicy Shrimp, p. 188) utilizes the fiery malagueta pepper and *dende* oil, so typical of Bahia, just as the recipe for Carurú (Bahian Shrimp Stew, p. 190) reflects its African origin with the use of okra, which was brought to South America by African slaves. Aficionados of Vatapá (Fish and Shrimp in Ginger-Peanut Sauce, p. 191) say that to experience it outside of Bahia is a pale comparison, but our recipe includes all of the traditional ingredients and doesn't stint on the chiles, so you can enjoy a truly fiery dish—even outside of Bahia!

A common denominator in tropical coast cookery is the addition of coconut milk and/or coconut water. Mariscos com Môlho Amendoim (Seafood in Hot Peanut Sauce, p. 192) uses coconut milk as well as grated coconut meat. Huachinango en Leche de Coco (Red Snapper Fillets in

Coconut Milk, p. 193) are cooked in coconut milk and then garnished with an additional cup of thick coconut milk. Coconut water, fruit, and chile peppers star in Pescado Guyanés al Curry (Guyanese Curried Fish, p. 194), with a dash of curry that reveals its East Indian roots.

The remaining shellfish recipes range from the simple, Ensalada de Camarones Picantes (Spicy Shrimp Salad, p. 196), to the complicated and elegant Mariscos con Frutas Citricas (Argentine Citrus Seafood, p. 198), and Camarones con Salsa de Almendras (Ecuadorian Shrimp in Almond Sauce, p. 200). Ostras da Panela (Brazilian-Style Oysters, p. 202) heat up with spicy malagueta chiles. From the coastal area of Peru, where fish is so plentiful, comes Arroz con Mariscos (Rice with Shrimp, Scallops, and Clams, p. 204). The ocean meets the mountains in the recipe Ocopa con Papas (Shrimp Sauce with Potatoes, p. 206), which includes ají chile peppers and walnuts.

Fresh Seafood Served Daily

"And when the Inca wished to eat fresh fish from the sea, and as it was seventy or eighty leagues from the coast to Cuzco . . . they were brought alive and twitching, which seems incredible over such a long distance over such rough and craggy roads, but they ran on foot, not on horseback, because they never had horses until the Spanish came to this country [Peru]."

—Martin de Murua

Ceviche de Corvina

(Peruvian Sea Bass Ceviche)

We have included several ceviche recipes from Peru in this book because some travelers claim that Peruvian ceviches are superior to those of Ecuador. The most popular fish used in Peru is sea bass, or grouper, although every type of fish and shellfish is used as well. The Peruvian ceviches are garnished with a few rounds of cooked corn and cooked slices of sweet potatoes.

1½	pounds sea bass fillets, cut into 1-inch pieces, or substitute swordfish	1	large onion, thinly sliced
1	teaspoon salt	1	cup fresh lemon juice
¼	teaspoon freshly ground black pepper	1	cup fresh lime juice
2	rocoto chiles, seeds and stems removed, thinly sliced into rings, or substitute 1 habanero or 3 jalapeños	1	clove garlic, minced
		1	pound sweet potatoes, peeled and cut into 1-inch thick slices
		3	ears fresh corn, cleaned and cut into 2-inch thick slices
1	teaspoon paprika		Bibb lettuce leaves

Place the cut and cleaned fish into a large glass or ceramic bowl and sprinkle with the salt and black pepper. Add half of the chile rings, paprika, onion, lemon juice, lime juice, and the garlic and mix lightly; cover the mixture and refrigerate for 3 to 5 hours until the fish is opaque.

About 30 minutes before serving the fish, cook the sweet potatoes in a large pot of boiling salted water for 12 minutes; then, add the corn to the pot and cook for 10 minutes more, until tender. Drain the vegetables and reserve them, at room temperature, for the garnish.

Drain the fish thoroughly in a colander and arrange the Bibb lettuce leaves on 4 dinner plates. Place the fish on the lettuce leaves and garnish with the reserved chile rings, and surround the fish with wheels of cooked sweet potatoes and corn.

Note: This recipe requires advance preparation.

Yield: 4 servings

Heat Scale: Medium

Chiles as Change

Food was not the only use for the beloved chiles of the Incas. According to historian L. E. Valcárcel, chile peppers were so highly valued in Incan society that they were probably used as currency. Since there were no coins or bills in those days, certain preferred products like chiles became part of a rudimentary monetary system. He noted that until the mid-twentieth century, shoppers in the plaza of Cuzco could buy goods with *rantii,* a handful of chiles.

Ceviche Mixto de Mariscos Peruano

(Peruvian Mixed Seafood Ceviche)

This particular ceviche is spicy because of the addition of a fair amount of crushed ajís (or whatever dried chiles you have available). The use of corn and sweet potatoes signal this dish as being very typically Peruvian. Serve it as an entree for lunch or dinner on those hot and sweltering days of summer.

¾ cup fresh lime juice

¾ cup fresh lemon juice

3 dried ají chiles, seeds and stems removed, crushed in a mortar, or substitute 2 New Mexican chiles (mild) or 6 piquins (hot)

1 clove garlic, minced

1 large red onion, sliced paper thin

1 teaspoon salt

¼ teaspoon freshly ground black pepper

½ pound cleaned shellfish (clams, oysters, mussels, or a mix)

1 teaspoon paprika (optional)

1 tablespoon chopped fresh parsley, Italian preferred

3 sweet potatoes, peeled and cut into 1-inch thick slices

3 ears fresh corn, cleaned and cut into 2-inch thick slices

4 Bibb lettuce leaves

Combine all the ingredients except the potatoes, corn, and lettuce in a large ceramic bowl, mix well, cover tightly, and refrigerate for 3 to 5 hours. If the citrus juice doesn't cover the fish, add more in equal amounts.

Just before serving, bring a large pot of salted water to a boil, and drop in the sweet potatoes and boil for 10 minutes. Drain the vegetables thoroughly.

Drain the fish in a colander to remove the marinade and arrange the fish on the lettuce on 4 dinner plates. Garnish with the sweet potatoes and the rounds of corn.

Note: This recipe requires advance preparation.

Yield: 4 servings

Heat Scale: Medium

The Conqueror's Spicy Fare

"But [the colonial Peruvians] were also fond of less nourishing but spicier dishes that were called *picantes,* containing hot peppers. Generally speaking, these were pre-cooked dishes that were bought in the *picanterías* run by the Indians. Among these highly seasoned dishes were *ajiaco,* a mixture of meat, fish and red pepper, and *ceviche,* cold raw fish cut up into small pieces and marinated for several hours in the juice of a green lemon. This dish was eaten with slices of raw onion, hot peppers, and boiled corn." —Jean Descola

Ceviche de Camarones

(Ecuadorian Marinated Shrimp)

This recipe comes from our friend, Loretta Salazar, who lived in Ecuador while she attended the university on an exchange program. The popcorn that is served on top of the ceviche is an American approximation probably of the toasted corn, or *cancha,* which is served over Peruvian ceviches. This ceviche is a quick one, if you use precooked, frozen mini-shrimp. Serve the ceviche on a bed of Bibb lettuce, garnished with black olives, sliced hard-boiled egg, feta cheese, a slice of cooked corn on the cob, and maybe some crusty bread for a very appetizing luncheon or light dinner.

2 pounds frozen cooked shrimp
1 medium red onion, sliced very thin
1 to 2 tablespoons chopped fresh ají chiles, or substitute yellow wax hot chiles or jalapeños
2 tablespoons chopped cilantro
3 medium tomatoes, finely chopped

3 tablespoons white wine vinegar
¾ cup fresh lemon juice
¾ cup fresh lime juice
½ cup good quality olive oil
½ teaspoon salt
   Bibb lettuce
2½ cups freshly popped popcorn

Pour the frozen shrimp into a colander and run cold water over them for a minute or two. Drain the shrimp thoroughly and then place them on paper towels to drain off the excess. Place the shrimp in a non-reactive bowl (such as Pyrex), add the remaining ingredients (except the lettuce and popcorn), mix lightly, and marinate the mixture in the refrigerator for 2 to 4 hours.

Drain the ceviche in a colander and serve on individual plates on beds of shredded lettuce, garnished with the warm popcorn.

Note: This recipe requires advance preparation.

Yield: 4 to 5 servings

Heat Scale: Mild

Ceviche con Naranja Agria
(Ceviche with Bitter Orange)

This recipe is another version of the Ecuadorian specialty. The fish can be served as an appetizer or as a main course for a refreshing summer meal. It is traditionally served with *maiz tostada* (toasted corn) or popcorn on the side. The lime juice "cooks" the fish, so no further actual cooking is necessary.

1½ pounds firm white fish fillets, snapper or catfish recommended

1 cup bitter (Seville) orange juice, or substitute ½ cup lemon juice mixed with ½ cup orange juice

1 cup fresh lime juice

1 onion, thinly sliced

1 cup chopped green bell pepper

1 cup chopped red bell pepper

1 habanero chile, seeds and stem removed, minced, or substitute 3 jalapeños

½ cup olive oil

1 clove garlic, minced

½ teaspoon salt

¼ teaspoon freshly ground black pepper

Garnishes: popcorn, red bell pepper rings, green bell pepper rings

Cut the cleaned fillets into thin, diagonal slices and place them in a large ceramic bowl. Pour the citrus juices over the fish, add the onion, chopped bell peppers, habanero, olive oil, garlic, salt, and ground black pepper, and mix gently to coat the fish. Cover the bowl tightly and refrigerate for at least 6 hours to "cook" the fish.

Drain the fish and arrange the slices on individual plates, garnishing with the popcorn and the pepper rings.

Note: This recipe requires advance preparation.

Yield: 4 to 5 servings

Heat Scale: Medium

Ceviche de Huachinango Marinado Estilo Peruano

(Marinated Snapper Peruvian-Style)

This ceviche is different from the others because the spicy chile-vegetable mixture is spread on the fish after it has finished "cooking." Add more chiles to pack more punch into your ceviche. And, speaking of packing a punch, Latin legends hold that ceviches are aphrodisiacs and will give a woman many sons.

2	pounds snapper or sole fillets, washed and cut into 1-inch strips	½	cup onion, finely chopped
½	cup fresh lime juice	2	cloves garlic, minced
½	cup fresh lemon juice	2	tablespoons cilantro or Italian parsley, minced
½	cup finely chopped red bell pepper	1	teaspoon salt
1	large tomato, peeled, seeded, and chopped	2	fresh ají chiles, seeds and stems removed, minced, or substitute yellow wax hot chiles or jalapeños
2	fresh pimientos, seeds and stems removed, finely chopped, or substitute red bell pepper	½	teaspoon sugar
		½	cup white wine vinegar

Place the fillets in a ceramic bowl, pour the lemon and lime juices over them, and mix the fish gently to coat with the juices. Cover the bowl tightly and refrigerate 8 hours or preferably overnight.

Mix the remaining ingredients together and allow the mixture to stand at room temperature for 1 hour.

Drain the fish and arrange it on lettuce leaves on 4 individual plates. Spread the chile mixture over the fish, dividing it evenly among the plates.

Note: This recipe requires advance preparation.

Yield: 4 servings

Heat Scale: Medium

Pescado Marinado Estilo Chileno

(Marinated Halibut Chilean-Style)

Because Chile has a 2,600-mile coastline, we would be remiss if we didn't include some fish recipes from that country. There is a minimum of grazing land in Chile, so instead of beef being the major source of protein, it is fish and shellfish. The wines of Chile are quite good, so be sure to include a chilled Chilean white wine when you serve this ceviche.

2 pounds halibut fillets, or substitute sole or flounder
1 cup fresh lemon juice
½ cup fresh orange juice
1 cup chopped onions
2 teaspoons Tabasco sauce, or substitute a Caribbean-style habanero sauce

1 fresh ají chile, seeds and stem removed, sliced into rings, or substitute yellow wax hot chile or jalapeño
1 teaspoon salt
2 tomatoes, peeled, seeded, and diced
Garnishes: tomato wedges and cilantro sprigs

Cut the fillets into 1-inch pieces, place them in a ceramic bowl, cover with the citrus juices, and toss them lightly to coat.

Add the remaining ingredients and mix gently. Cover the bowl tightly and refrigerate overnight. Drain off some of the juice and arrange the fillets on lettuce leaves on 4 individual plates and garnish with the tomatoes and the cilantro.

Note: This recipe requires advance preparation.

Yield: 4 servings

Heat Scale: Medium

Ceviche de Ostras

(Guatemalan Marinated Oysters)

Although the triad of corn, beans, and rice reign supreme in Guatemala, there are also many exotic dishes, perhaps traces of Mayan foraging. This dish intrigues because the habaneros add the heat, and the mint provides an interesting twist on the more traditional cilantro.

48	oysters, shucked	3	tablespoons finely chopped fresh mint leaves
½	cup fresh lime juice	½	teaspoon salt
½	cup fresh lemon juice	¼	teaspoon freshly ground black pepper
3	tomatoes, peeled, seeded, and chopped		Garnishes: lettuce leaves, fresh mint sprigs, tomato wedges
1	cup chopped onion		
1	fresh habanero chile, seeds and stem removed, minced, or substitute 3 jalapeños		

Place the oysters in a large ceramic bowl and cover with the lime and lemon juices. Cover tightly and refrigerate overnight.

Drain the oysters and reserve ¼ cup of the juice. Add the remaining ingredients to the oysters, along with the reserved juice, and toss the mixture gently.

Line 6 plates with the lettuce leaves, arrange 8 oysters with their marinade on the lettuce on each plate, and garnish with the fresh mint and the tomato wedges.

Note: This recipe requires advance preparation.

Yield: 6 servings

Heat Scale: Medium

Escabeche de Pescado

(Peruvian Fish in Ají Sauce)

Mary Dempsey, who wrote about spicy Peruvian dishes for *Chile Pepper* magazine, observed: "As befitting a nation with miles of Pacific coastline, many dishes in Peru use seafood. *Escabeche* is cold fried fish in a marinade of onions and hot peppers. Serve this with boiled sweet potatoes, corn on the cob, and a crisp salad."

6	fillets white fish, such as catfish Flour	2	onions, cut into thin wedges
2	tablespoons vegetable oil Ground cumin, salt, and pepper to taste	2	fresh ají chiles, seeds and stems removed, cut into thin strips, or substitute yellow wax hot chiles, red serranos, or jalapeños
4	fresh ají chiles, seeds and stems removed, or substitute red serranos or jalapeños	⅓	cup vinegar Lettuce
2	cloves garlic, peeled		

Roll the fish fillets in flour and fry them in the oil until golden brown, about 10 minutes, turning occasionally. Remove the fish, drain on paper towels, and season with cumin, salt, and pepper. Set aside to cool.

Grind together the 4 ajís and 2 cloves of garlic in a blender. In the same pan, fry the chile and garlic mixture until golden, then add the onions, chile strips, and vinegar, adding more oil if necessary. Sauté for 5 minutes.

Place the fried fish fillets on a bed of lettuce and cover with the *escabeche* sauce. Serve warm or at room temperature.

Yield: 6 servings

Heat Scale: Hot

Escabeche de Huachinango

(Red Snapper Escabeche)

This Peruvian dish is popular throughout South America, probably because of the great availability of fresh fish. Even the Inca nobility, high up in the Andes, had access to fresh fish because of the intricate system of runners that was set up. And when royalty wanted it, the runners brought snow. The technique of cooking this dish is Spanish, although New World cooks have added their own special touches and ingredients. The use of achiote adds a slight musky taste as well as coloring the dish yellow.

3	pounds red snapper fillets, or substitute any firm white fish
1	teaspoon salt
¼	teaspoon freshly ground black pepper
1	cup flour
2	teaspoons paprika
3	tablespoons butter or vegetable oil
½	cup olive oil
2	cloves garlic, minced
½	teaspoon achiote (annatto seeds)

3	onions, sliced into ¼-inch rings
2	fresh ají or rocoto chiles, seeds and stems removed, chopped fine, or substitute yellow wax hot chiles or jalapeños
¼	teaspoon oregano or thyme
¾	cup white wine vinegar
	Garnishes: cheese (Muenster or Monterey Jack), black olives, cooked corn on the cob, cut into 2-inch rounds, sliced hard-boiled eggs, lettuce leaves

Sprinkle the fish with the salt and pepper. Place the flour and the paprika into a large plastic bag and dredge the fillets, shaking off any excess flour.

Melt the butter in a skillet and sauté the fish until it is lightly browned on both sides. Remove the fish to a warm platter and keep warm.

In a clean, large skillet, heat the olive oil and add the garlic, achiote, onions, and chiles, and sauté until the onions are soft. Sprinkle in the oregano and the vinegar, stirring until the mixture is hot. Pour the mixture over the fish and serve. Garnish with some or all of the suggested garnishes.

Yield: 6 to 8 servings

Heat Scale: Medium

Eja

(Bahian Snapper with Malagueta Shrimp Sauce)

This recipe is from Tita Libín, who has spent much time studying the foods, the gods, and the lore of Bahia, and wrote on the subject for *Chile Pepper*. Bahia is the homeland of the Orixas, the Brazilian gods, where the African religions blended with Catholicism, and each Orixa has a favorite food and specific characteristics. Ye Manja is the Queen of the Sea; her Catholic counterpart is Our Lady of the Sailors and Our Lady of the Divine Conception. Her colors are blue and white, her special day is Saturday, the greeting is "Ooo La," her element is water, and her favorite food is Eja, or Bahian snapper.

¼ cup dried shrimp (available in Latin or Asian markets)

8 dried malagueta chiles, stems and seeds removed, crushed, divided in half, or substitute piquins

1 cup lemon juice

4 red snapper fillets, ½-inch thick, or substitute any firm white fish

3 tablespoons olive oil

1 cup chopped onions

¼ teaspoon freshly ground black pepper

Salt to taste

Combine the shrimp, half of the chiles, and lemon juice in a glass or ceramic bowl. Marinate the fish in this mixture for 1 hour. Remove the fish, pat dry, and reserve the marinade. Heat the oil and fry the fish on both sides until cooked, about 5 minutes per side. Remove the fish and keep warm in the oven on low heat.

Add the onions to the frying pan and sauté until soft. Stir in the reserved marinade, marinated shrimp, remaining chiles, and black pepper. Simmer for a couple of minutes to thicken and season to taste with salt.

Place the fish fillets on a serving platter, top with the shrimp sauce, and serve.

Note: This recipe requires advance preparation.

Yield: 4 servings

Heat Scale: Hot

Bobó de Camarão

(Bahian Spicy Shrimp)

This recipe is the food of another Bahian Orixa, Nana, the oldest and kindest of all sacred women. Tita Libín found that Nana's Catholic counterpart is Saint Ann, her colors are blue and white, her sacred day is Tuesday, the greeting is "Saluba," her element is sweet water, and her food is Bobó de Camarão.

6 dried malagueta chiles, seeds and stems removed, or substitute piquins	1 tablespoon palm oil or substitute vegetable oil with 1 teaspoon ground paprika
3 tablespoons olive oil	½ teaspoon ground cinnamon
½ cup chopped onion	¼ teaspoon ground cloves
¼ cup finely chopped celery	¼ teaspoon ground ginger
6 cloves garlic, chopped	3 tablespoons lemon juice
1 cup chopped pimiento, seeds and stems removed, or substitute red bell pepper	Salt and freshly ground black pepper to taste
4 cups shrimp, peeled and deveined	¼ cup finely chopped fresh cilantro
2 cups chopped tomatoes	6 cups cooked rice
1 cup coconut milk	

Cover the chiles with hot water for 15 minutes or until soft. Remove and chop.

Heat the oil and sauté the onions until soft. Add the celery, garlic, chiles, and pimiento and continue to sauté for an additional 5 minutes. Stir in the shrimp, and sauté until they turn pink, then remove and reserve.

Add the tomatoes, coconut milk, palm oil, and spices. Bring to a boil, reduce the heat and simmer until the mixture thickens, about 10 minutes.

Return the shrimp, stir in the lemon juice and season with salt and pepper. Garnish with the cilantro and immediately serve on top of the rice.

Yield: 6 to 8 servings

Heat Scale: Medium

Carurú

(Bahian Shrimp Stew)

The African influence is evident in this dish—the *dende* oil and the okra were brought to Brazil by the African slaves. The chile of choice for the spice in this dish is the malagueta. Many of the ingredients can be found in Latin and Asian markets, such as the *dende* oil, manioc flour, and the dried shrimp. Serve this dish with white rice or any of the rice dishes in Chapter 8.

1	pound okra, chopped	1	teaspoon paprika
3	cups water	2	cloves garlic, minced
½	teaspoon salt	½	cup crushed cashew nuts
¼	pound dried shrimp, shelled	¼	cup peanut butter
1	pound fresh shrimp, shelled and deveined	3	small dried malagueta chiles, stems and seeds removed and crushed, or substitute piquins
3	tablespoons *dende* (palm) oil or peanut oil infused with 2 teaspoons paprika	½	teaspoon freshly grated ginger
1	cup chopped onion	¼	cup manioc flour or farina, for thickening

Place the okra in a saucepan with the water and salt. Bring the water to a boil, turn the heat down to a simmer, and cook, uncovered, for 10 minutes.

Grind the dried shrimp and half of the fresh shrimp together in a food processor or a blender. Add this mixture to the simmering okra along with the oil, onion, paprika, garlic, and cashew nuts, stirring for a minute.

Then, add the peanut butter, chiles, and ginger. Stir this mixture constantly for 2 to 3 minutes, until it starts to thicken a little. Add the remaining fresh shrimp and cook for 10 to 15 minutes, stirring gently. If the mixture seems too thick, add water, a little at a time. Conversely, if the mixture isn't thickening, stir in a little manioc flour.

Yield: 4 to 6 servings

Heat Scale: Medium

Vatapá
(Fish and Shrimp in Ginger-Peanut Sauce)

This recipe is typical of Bahia; it has the African influences of palm oil, red chiles (usually malaguetas), bananas, and coconuts. The food of Salvador, the capital, also plays a central role in Jorge Amado's novels, including *Doña Flor and Her Two Husbands*. Vatapá is the food of Ogun, the Bahian Orixa of iron and war. His Catholic counterpart is Saint Anthony, and his color is navy blue. This is a different version of the dish found in Chapter 4.

1 pound white fish fillets, cut in 2-inch cubes	½ cup chopped cashew nuts
½ cup dried shrimp, finely chopped	1 cup chunky peanut butter
2 to 3 tablespoons olive oil	2 slices bread, soaked in water
¼ cup chopped green onion	½ teaspoon freshly ground black pepper
1 small onion, finely chopped	½ teaspoon ground cloves
1 teaspoon minced fresh ginger	1 tablespoon palm oil or substitute vegetable oil with 1 teaspoon ground paprika
2 cups chopped tomatoes	
2 teaspoons crushed malagueta chile, or substitute piquin	2 cups water
1 cup coconut milk	¼ cup chopped fresh cilantro

Sauté the fish and shrimp in the oil in a Dutch oven until just done, about 5 to 6 minutes. Remove and keep warm.

Add the green onion, onion, and ginger and sauté until soft. Stir in the tomatoes and simmer for 5 minutes. Add the remaining ingredients, except the cilantro. Bring to a boil, reduce the heat and simmer, uncovered, for 15 minutes or until the sauce has thickened.

Return the fish and shrimp. Add the cilantro and heat through. Serve with rice and beans.

Yield: 4 servings

Heat Scale: Medium

Mariscos com Môlho Amendoim

(Seafood in Hot Peanut Sauce)

Nancy Gerlach, food editor of *Chile Pepper* magazine, collected this recipe in Rio de Janeiro. Serve it with Camotes Fritos (p. 221), fried sweet potatoes, and any rice dish from Chapter 8.

1	pound white fish fillets, cut in 3-inch pieces	2	teaspoons coriander seeds
3	to 4 tablespoons olive oil	2	large tomatoes, peeled and chopped
1	pound raw shrimp, shelled and deveined	1	cup chicken broth
1	small onion, finely chopped	1	cup coconut milk
1	small green bell pepper, stem and seeds removed, chopped	½	cup chopped peanuts
1	tablespoon grated ginger	1	cup grated coconut
1	habanero chile, stem and seeds removed, minced, or substitute 3 jalapeños		Chopped fresh cilantro

Lightly brown the fish in the oil. Remove and keep warm. Add the shrimp and sauté until just pink, remove and keep warm. Add the onion, pepper, ginger, and habanero and sauté until the onions are soft. Stir in the coriander, tomatoes, broth, and coconut milk. Simmer the sauce for 15 to 20 minutes. Place in a blender or food processor and puree until smooth.

Return the sauce to the pan and add the peanuts and coconut and simmer until the sauce is slightly thickened. Return the fish and shrimp to the sauce and heat through.

Garnish with the cilantro and serve.

Yield: 4 to 6 servings

Heat Scale: Medium

Huachinango en Leche de Coco

(Red Snapper Fillets in Coconut Milk)

Seafood reigns supreme on the Caribbean coast of Colombia, and when it is cooked with coconut milk, it yields a delicate, flavorful dish. So, as not to overpower the delicacy of this dish, we suggest serving it with cooked rice and a lightly dressed green salad.

3	pounds red snapper fillets, cut into 6 pieces, or substitute grouper or any firm, white fish	1	cup finely chopped onion
1	teaspoon salt	2	fresh habanero chiles, seeds and stems removed, minced, or substitute 3 jalapeños
	Freshly ground black pepper	3	cups coconut milk
3	tomatoes, peeled, seeded, and diced	1	cup thick coconut milk (see Note)

Place the fillets in a single layer in a large skillet and salt and pepper them. Spread the tomatoes, onions, and habanero peppers evenly over the fish. Pour in the 3 cups of coconut milk and simmer for 10 minutes. Remove the fish to a warm platter and keep warm. Reserve the remaining coconut milk in the skillet.

Bring the reserved milk to a slow boil and cook it down, stirring, until about 1 cup remains. Add the thick coconut milk and heat through. Pour the mixture through a sieve, onto the fish on the platter. Serve immediately.

Note: To make thick coconut milk, grate about a cup of fresh coconut meat into a small bowl and pour 1¼ cups hot water over it. Allow the mixture to sit for 15 minutes. Then, press this mixture through a fine sieve, removing as much liquid as possible and discard the coconut meat. The result should be about 1 cup of thick coconut milk.

Yield: 6 servings

Heat Scale: Medium

Pescado Guyanés al Curry
(Guyanese Curried Fish)

The Guyanese often use canned salmon in this dish, but we suggest other flavorful fish, cooked and flaked. The addition of hot sauce and curry powder suggests this recipe has its roots with the East Indian laborers who were brought to the Caribbean. In keeping with a curry dinner, we suggest serving it with white rice and condiments such as chopped salted peanuts, pickle relish, chopped hard-boiled eggs, mango chutney, and finely diced cucumber.

4	whole fresh coconuts
2	tablespoons butter
1	cup finely diced onion
2	cloves garlic, minced
¼	teaspoon freshly ground black pepper
2	teaspoons habanero hot pepper sauce
1	tablespoon curry powder, preferably Indian
5	to 6 tablespoons flour

2½	cups coconut water (liquid from inside fresh coconuts)
1	pound cooked white fish, such as flounder or catfish, flaked
¼	cup chopped mango chutney
¼	teaspoon salt
2	tablespoons fresh lime juice
¾	cup diced partially ripe papaya
¼	cup flour, or more
2	to 3 tablespoons water

Saw the tops off the coconuts and reserve the coconut water. Remove the coconut meat from the tops, grate it, and toast it in a 200°F oven, stirring often, until the coconut meat is lightly toasted. Reserve.

Melt the butter in a large skillet and sauté the onion and the garlic until they are soft. Add the black pepper, the habanero pepper sauce, and the curry powder and cook for 5 minutes over low heat, stirring constantly so the mixture doesn't burn. Sprinkle in the flour and blend thoroughly.

Add the reserved coconut water to the curry mixture, stirring constantly until the sauce is thick and smooth.

Then add the flaked fish, chutney, salt, lime juice, and diced papaya, mixing thoroughly but gently. Spoon this mixture into the coconut shells and replace the tops.

Make a thick paste with the flour and the water. Use this paste on the outside of the coconut tops to seal them.

Place the filled coconuts in a large baking dish and stabilize them by placing them in metal rings (such as tuna fish cans with the tops and bottoms cut out. Bake in a preheated 350°F oven for 1 hour. Crack open the coconut tops and serve with the reserved toasted coconut and suggested accompaniments.

Note: If you are using fresh fish, cook it briefly in a little water and use this water as part of the liquid measurement.

Yield: 4 servings

Heat Scale: Medium

Ensalada de Camarones Picantes

(Spicy Shrimp Salad)

While visiting friends in Costa Rica, we were served a version of this as a luncheon entree. Since Costa Ricans generally don't eat their food terribly spicy, we think this dish may have been an invention of our hosts, using the best of the local vegetables and shrimp.

20 large shrimp, cooked, peeled, deveined, and chilled

1⅓ cups hearts of palm, cut into chunks

2 fresh tomatoes, sliced

½ cup sliced scallion

1 fresh habanero chile, seeds and stem removed, minced, or substitute 3 jalapeños

Bibb lettuce leaves

Juice of 2 fresh limes

¼ cup olive oil

Salt and freshly ground black pepper to taste

Toss the shrimp, hearts of palm, tomatoes, scallions, and the habanero together in a large bowl.

Arrange the lettuce leaves on 4 plates and mound the shrimp mixture on top. Combine the lime juice and olive oil and drizzle the mixture over the salads. Season with the salt and pepper.

Yield: 4 servings

Heat Scale: Medium

The Patron Saint of Ceviche

"Saint Anthony, who presides over fishermen and cooks alike, usually is represented in the Brazilian kitchen by a small painted wooden statue that looks down from his little shelf with special benignity when *roballo* (a sea pike) or pompano is ceremoniously laid out on the board and the dressing of it begun, while the tail is being wrapped in a bit of oiled paper to keep it intact and the head perhaps is being tied with string to keep the jaws from sagging open in cooking. For no Latin would spoil the looks of a roast fish by cutting off its most decorative features." —Cora, Rose, and Bob Brown

Mariscos con Frutas Citricas

(Argentine Citrus Seafood)

Many Argentinian stews call for fresh fruit and even dried fruit. This spicy, creamed seafood dish is very elegant and makes a gorgeous presentation dish. Accompany with a simple green salad and a chilled Argentinian white wine.

2	cups long-grained white rice	3	tablespoons finely chopped green bell pepper
½	cup butter	3	pounds lobster, cooked and cubed
1	2-inch thread of saffron		
½	teaspoon salt	1	pound medium shrimp, cooked, peeled, and deveined
4	cups chicken stock, boiling		
¼	cup chopped pimientos, or substitute red bell pepper	½	pound crabmeat, cooked and flaked
½	cup cooked tiny green peas	3	oranges, peeled and thinly sliced into circles
2	tablespoons flour		
1½	cups milk	2	ripe avocados, peeled and sliced
1	tablespoon Louisiana-style hot sauce		
¼	cup minced onion	2	grapefruits, peeled and sectioned
2	cloves garlic, minced	16	lime wedges

Combine the rice, 3 tablespoons of butter, saffron, salt, and the boiling chicken stock. Bring to a boil, reduce the heat to a simmer, cover, and simmer for 20 minutes. When the rice is tender, stir in the pimientos and the peas and keep the rice warm.

Melt 2 tablespoons of butter in a large, heavy saucepan and sprinkle in the flour and stir for 30 seconds until it is well blended with the butter, taking care not to burn the mixture. Add the milk, all at once, and the hot sauce, stirring constantly until the mixture starts to thicken. If the mixture is not smooth, beat it with a whisk. Then, remove the cream sauce from the heat and set aside.

Melt 3 tablespoons of butter in a large skillet, and add the onion, garlic, and bell pepper, and sauté for 30 seconds. Then, add the lobster, shrimp, and crabmeat and toss the mixture lightly. Add the cream sauce to the seafood mixture and heat slowly, until the mixture is hot. Serve the creamed seafood over the cooked rice and garnish with the oranges, avocados, grapefruit, and lime wedges.

Yield: 8 servings

Heat Scale: Medium

Camarones con Salsa de Almendras

(Ecuadorian Shrimp in Almond Sauce)

This recipe appears in many different forms in both Ecuador and Chile—each claiming it as its own, which is not unlikely as both countries have an abundance of seafood in general, and shrimp in particular. The almonds and the addition of cream make this a very rich dish. We suggest an accompaniment of cooked quinoa, a simply dressed green salad, and a good chilled white Chilean wine.

1½ cups water
2   celery stalks, cut into 3-inch pieces
½   teaspoon pickling spice
½   cup dry white wine
½   teaspoon salt
2   pounds shrimp, shelled and deveined
1¼ cups day-old, good white bread, diced
1¼ cups milk
¼   cup butter
2   cups diced onion

2   cloves garlic, minced
¼   teaspoon freshly ground black pepper
1   teaspoon dried, crushed ají chile, or substitute New Mexican
1   teaspoon paprika
½   cup cream
2   tablespoons olive oil
1   cup ground almonds
    Garnishes: hard-boiled egg slices and grated Parmesan cheese

Bring the water to a boil in a large pot, and add the celery, pickling spice, white wine, salt, and the shrimp, and cook over medium heat for 3 minutes. Drain the shrimp and reserve 1 cup of the cooking liquid. Pick out any large pieces of the pickling spice that remain on the shrimp.

Soak the bread in the milk for 10 to 12 minutes and then mash the bread until it is smooth.

Melt the butter in a skillet and sauté the onions and the garlic until the onions are softened. Add the black pepper, crushed chile, and the paprika and mix.

Squeeze some of the milk out of the bread and add the bread to the onion mixture along with the cream and cook over medium heat for 3 to 5 minutes, stirring constantly until the mixture is thickened. Mix in the olive oil and the ground almonds and cook for 2 minutes, stirring. If the mixture seems too thick, add some of the reserved shrimp stock to thin it. Add the shrimp and heat through.

Serve the shrimp on warmed plates and garnish with the hard-boiled egg slices and grated Parmesan cheese.

Yield: 6 servings

Heat Scale: Mild

Ostras da Panela

(Brazilian-Style Oysters)

This recipe is rich, tasty, and reminiscent of a New England chowder—except that few New Englanders ever put malagueta chiles in their chowder! Until now, that is. The chiles heat up the oysters, but the cream tends to act as a neutralizer. Since this dish is so rich, keep the accompaniments simple: sliced fresh tomatoes, excellent bread, and a cold white wine.

¼ cup butter	½ teaspoon salt
1 tablespoon Worcestershire sauce	2 dozen shucked oysters, with their juice
1 tablespoon fresh lemon juice	1 cup cream
1 teaspoon crushed malagueta chile, or substitute piquin	1 16-ounce can of hearts of palm, drained and rinsed, and cut into ½-inch rounds
3 tablespoons minced celery leaves	1 tablespoon butter
¼ teaspoon freshly ground black pepper	2 tablespoons chopped cilantro or Italian parsley

Melt the butter in a medium saucepan and add the Worcestershire sauce, lemon juice, crushed chile, celery leaves, black pepper, and salt. Add the oysters and their juice and bring to a boil. Immediately lower the heat to a simmer and cook for 2 minutes.

Add the cream and heat through, but do not allow the mixture to boil.

Divide the hearts of palm among 4 bowls, add the oyster mixture, and top each bowl with a dab of butter and a sprinkling of cilantro.

Yield: 4 servings

Heat Scale: Medium

The Gigantic, Endangered Amazon Fish

"Over much of the Amazon proper, the growing number of gigantic dams and rapidly escalating pollution of major rivers have already all but wiped out the huge, but harmless *pirarucu,* once a staple of the region because it routinely weighs four hundred pounds. In the early 20th century, trade in dried or salted *pirarucu* was still such that it was commonly referred to as the fresh-water cod." —Alain Gheerbrant

Arroz con Mariscos

(Rice with Shrimp, Scallops, and Clams)

Even though Peru claims this recipe, variations are found throughout the coastal areas of Ecuador and Chile, where fish and shellfish abound. In a salute to Chile, serve a chilled Chilean white wine with this dish. A bean dish from Chapter 8, a fresh green salad, and some sliced tomatoes will make this meal a feast.

1 tablespoon olive oil	2 cloves garlic, minced
18 medium shrimp, cleaned, shells reserved	2 fresh ají or rocoto chiles, seeds and stems removed, minced, or substitute yellow wax hot chiles or jalapeños
1 sprig parsley	
2 onion slices	
¼ teaspoon thyme	2 cups long-grain white rice
4 whole black peppercorns	2 tablespoons chopped cilantro or Italian parsley
4 cups water	
½ to 1 cup clam broth	½ pound fresh scallops
½ teaspoon salt	14 cherrystone clams, shelled and washed
3 tablespoons olive oil	
1 cup chopped onion	14 oysters, shucked and washed

Heat 1 tablespoon of olive oil in a small heavy saucepan, add the shrimp shells, and stir them in the oil until they turn pink. Add the parsley, onion, thyme, peppercorns, and the water. Bring this mixture to a boil, then lower the heat to a simmer, cover, and cook for 30 minutes. Strain the liquid and measure; there should be 3 to 3½ cups. Add enough of the clam liquid to make 4 cups total. Season with the salt and set aside.

Heat 3 tablespoons of olive oil in a heavy skillet. Sauté the onion, garlic, and the chiles only until the onion is soft. Transfer the sautéed mixture to a casserole, leaving as much oil as possible in the skillet; if there isn't

2 to 3 tablespoons, add more oil. Add the rice and sauté over low heat for 1 minute, stirring frequently. Add the rice to the casserole and add the reserved shrimp stock, and bring the mixture to a boil. Reduce the heat to low, cover the casserole, and simmer for 20 minutes, until the rice is tender and the liquid is absorbed. Stir the cilantro, the reserved shrimp, scallops, and clams into the rice, cover, and cook for 3 to 5 minutes, until the shrimp is pink. Then, add the oysters and cook for 1 minute.

Yield: 6 to 8 servings

Heat Scale: Medium

Ocopa con Papas
(Shrimp Sauce with Potatoes)

This Peruvian dish has everything—shrimp, potatoes, and chile. However, the amount of chiles used means it is going to be a very hot and spicy dish, very typical of Peru, where people consume vast quantities of chiles just like the Bahians. Try serving this dish on a hot summer night, along with a fresh green salad, and watch your guests perspire their way to coolness. This is a variation of Potato Sauce Arequipa-Style (p. 20).

6   dried ají chile pods, seeds and stems removed, torn into small pieces, or substitute New Mexican
    Warm water for soaking
½   teaspoon salt
18 medium shrimp, washed
    Water just to cover
½   cup plus 2 tablespoons olive oil
½   cup chopped onion

2   cloves garlic, chopped
½   teaspoon marjoram
3   tablespoons fresh parsley
2   to 4 tablespoons cottage cheese
¼   cup chopped walnuts
4   potatoes, boiled, peeled, and sliced
    Garnish: 2 hard-boiled eggs, sliced; minced cilantro

Soak the chiles in the warm water and salt for 1 hour. Rinse the chiles, drain them in a colander, and set aside.

In a medium saucepan, cover the shrimp with water and boil them for 5 to 6 minutes. Reserve the cooking water and clean the shrimp. Place the cleaned shrimp in a food processor.

Heat 2 tablespoons of the olive oil in a small skillet and sauté the onion and the garlic for 1 minute. Add the sautéed mixture to the shrimp, along with the chiles, marjoram, parsley, cottage cheese, and the walnuts.

Puree the shrimp mixture, adding the remaining oil and shrimp water to thin the sauce a little. The mixture should be a thick and creamy but pourable sauce.

Arrange the sliced potatoes on a platter or on individual plates and pour the shrimp sauce over the potatoes. Garnish with the hard-boiled egg slices and sprinkle the minced cilantro over the top of sauce.

Yield: 4 servings

Heat Scale: Hot

Anyone for Skinny Dipping in the Amazon?

"Stinging rays *(tapaderas)* and cannibal fishes (the *piranhas*) were a menace. Sting-ray spines, able to cause severe wounds, were used for weapon points and for tatooing. *Piranha* were, and are, greatly feared, for they could snip off a finger, but the flesh was good, and the sharp teeth were used for cutting instruments. Another fish, minute in size, the *cañero* or *candiru,* hooks itself into the vagina or the penis aperture of a bather. Protective devices were often used." —Carleton Beals

8

Papas y Mas
Andean Hot Potatoes
to Jungle Vegetables

W hen the Old World explorers arrived in Latin America, they found a vast array of foods that were new to them: tomatoes, corn, potatoes, chile peppers, avocados, cassava, squash, peanuts, and quinoa, to name a few.

Some dominant staples included: maize (corn), potatoes, quinoa, and rice. Maize and potatoes were important sources of carbohydrates and are frequently compared to the status of rice in Asia and taro in the Pacific. In many parts of the world, except Latin America, a corn-based diet usually meant the onset of pellagra—a nutrient deficiency.

However, in Latin America, pellagra was nonexistent because of the way corn was treated; corn kernels were soaked and boiled in water with wood ash, an alkali that released the nicotinic acid present in the corn. The corn kernels could then be used as a kind of hominy, or could be dried and ground into flour for masa harina, which is used for the making of tortillas.

High in the Andes, corn does not grow well because of the cold weather, so it was here that potatoes became the important staple food. The Andean area produces more than 200 varieties of potatoes, and some of these relatives can be found in North American markets; they range in color from bright yellow to red to purple, and some have odd shapes. Potatoes cannot be directly imported from Peru to the United States because of agricultural restrictions.

Potatoes sustained the Incas well, but the potato was shunned by the Europeans, who thought they were poisonous because they belong to the Nightshade family, as does belladonna. Nietzsche wrote: "A diet that consists predominately of potatoes leads to the use of liquor." Even though Thomas Jefferson planted potatoes on his land, most North Americans in the eighteenth and nineteenth centuries looked askance at them. "They should be grown near hog-pens as a convenience towards feeding the hogs," suggested the instructions in the *Farmer's Manual*.

Long before North Americans were feeding potatoes to their hogs, the Incas had created the first freeze-dried product: potatoes. These potatoes, called *chuño*, keep indefinitely and become hard and light when they are freeze-dried; they are frequently described as small, gray stones and can be found in Latin American markets. They are added to stews where they are rehydrated and add a nourishing touch, as well as a delicious taste.

Protein-rich quinoa is another contribution of the Andes area, and it balanced the intake of carbohydrates. It was called the mother grain by the Incas, and it has flourished in cultivation for over 5,000 years. Quinoa was the grain that accompanied the Incan armies during their conquests. Now, it is sometimes called the grain of the future—what a leap in culinary history! It is still an important food in South American cuisine and often takes the place of meat in the diets of the peasants.

Quinoa is available in health food stores, whole food markets, and by mail order. We recently purchased the whole grain in a co-op store here in Albuquerque, as well as some quinoa pasta; both are very good. Quinoa is a boon for people who have a wheat intolerance because it is available as quinoa linguini and other shapes and forms and can be used as an alternative to durum semolina pasta.

Compared to corn, potatoes, and quinoa, rice has to be considered a relative newcomer to Latin American cuisine, and one that has been enthusiastically embraced. Rice was introduced from the Old World by the Spanish and the Portuguese in the sixteenth century, and it flourished in the warm, steamy lowlands of the coastal areas. Today, rice is used all over Latin America; however, it is particularly popular in such countries as Brazil and Costa Rica, where it shares an equal place with maize.

Chile peppers, beans, avocados, pumpkins, squash, and sweet potatoes were some of the vegetables available to early Latin Americans. These indigenous vegetables balanced out the nutrients found in rice, corn, and potatoes. Brazil nuts and peanuts (actually a legume) were common as well, and walnuts were introduced with the Spanish conquest.

Our first three rice recipes are from the tropical lowlands, and all three use coconut in one form or another. Arroz de Huaca (Oxala's Rice, p. 212) is a Bahian recipe that contains coconut milk and malagueta chiles, two common ingredients found in Bahia. Arroz con Leche de Coco y Chile (Coconut-Chile Rice, p. 213) is representative of Belize with its abundant coconuts and habanero chiles. Coconut, raisins, and chiles star in Arroz con Coco y Pasas (Colombian Coconut Rice with Raisins, p. 214); the recipe is indicative of the Spanish-Indian cuisine found in Colombia. Costa Rican Gallo Pinto (Beans and Rice, p. 216) is, without a doubt, the national dish of Costa Rica; it is eaten every day and at any hour.

Frijoles Negros (Brazilian Black Beans, p. 218) are nutritious, as well as hot and spicy. The high protein content in beans have sustained the poorer people of Latin America; however, black beans hold great favor in Brazil, and its national dish is centered on them. A rich, interesting dish is Frijoles Negros en Salsa de Nueces (Black Beans in Walnut Sauce, p. 220).

A contemporary twist on sweet potatoes is found in Camotes Fritos (Hot Fried Sweet Potatoes, p. 221), jazzed up with chile powder; try substituting these in place of ordinary french fries. Llapingachos (Ecuadorian Spiced Potato Cakes, p. 222) offer a traditional and clever use for mashed potatoes, cheese, and chiles. Papas Arequipeña (Fiery Potatoes in Peanut and Cheese Sauce, p. 223) is a Peruvian-style potato dish. Papas Huancaino Numero Uno (Potatoes Huancayo-Style, p. 224) is substantial enough to be a meal in itself. Two kinds of cheese are used in the recipe for Papas Huancaino Numero Dos (Potatoes Huancayo-Style, p. 226), and it is just as delicious as the previous recipe.

The very versatile grain, quinoa, is represented in two recipes; Ensalada con Quinoa de Peru (Peruvian Quinoa Salad, p. 228) is full of fresh vegetables and is dressed with chiles and lime juice. The second recipe, Ensalada con

Quinoa de Bolivia (Bolivian Quinoa Salad, p. 230), is accented with the tastes of chile, walnuts, and raisins.

Next, we use a wide variety of vegetables, beginning with Humitas con Achiote (Pureed Corn with Annatto, p. 232), which can be compared to a mini-tamale. Cabbage, that inexpensive and versatile vegetable, becomes a substantial side dish in Guiso de Repollo (Bolivian Cabbage in Tomato Sauce, p. 234), combining cabbage with tomatoes and potatoes. Repôlho com Vinho (Chile-Spiced Cabbage with Wine, p. 235) becomes a fiery side dish with the addition of habanero chile peppers. Paltas Rellenas (Peruvian Stuffed Avocados, p. 236) are filled with a variety of ingredients, then topped with a shrimp garnish. Picante de Aguacates (Spicy Chilean Avocados, p. 237) is a lighter side dish stuffed with egg yolks, chiles, cilantro, and onions. A rich and spicy dish, Hongos con Chile y Queso (Mushrooms with Chile and Cheese, p. 238) contains tomatoes, ají chiles, and a splash of fresh cilantro. Ají chiles and leeks add a different taste to Habas con Ajís (Lima Beans with Ají Chiles, p. 239) that is topped with citrus zest. Chayote con Ajís (Chayote Squash Sautéed with Ají Chiles, p. 240) contains two standard Latin ingredients—chiles and corn, and it is dressed with cilantro and Parmesan cheese.

Arroz de Huaca

(Oxala's Rice)

Oxala is the highest Orixa of the Bahian gods of Brazil, the king of the universe. His Catholic counterpart is Jesus. His other specific characteristics are day, Friday; color, white; greeting, "Exe e baba"; element, the whole universe. This is His rice—and the recipe is from Tita Libín.

½ cup minced onion
1   dried malagueta chile, stem and seeds removed, crushed, or substitute piquin, Thai, or Japanese

2   tablespoons olive oil
1   cup white rice
½ cup boiling water
1½ cups coconut milk

Sauté the onion and chile in the oil until the onions are soft. Add the rice and continue to sauté until the rice turns opaque.

Combine the water and coconut milk and bring to a boil. Add the rice mixture and bring back to a boil. Lower the heat, cover, and simmer for 30 minutes or until the rice is tender.

Fluff the rice with a fork before serving.

Yield: 4 servings

Heat Scale: Medium

Arroz con Leche de Coco y Chile
(Coconut-Chile Rice)

Coconuts are plentiful in Belize and all along the Caribbean coast of Central and South America. This Belizean recipe is from *Chile Pepper* magazine food editor Nancy Gerlach, who was almost beaned on the head by a coconut while sitting on the porch of our temporary residence on Ambergris Caye.

1 cup grated fresh coconut

2 tablespoons butter

1 small onion, finely chopped

1 habanero chile, stem and seeds removed, minced, or substitute 3 jalapeños

1 cup white rice

1 cup coconut milk

1½ cups chicken stock

Minced cilantro for garnish

Sauté the grated coconut in the butter for a couple of minutes or until it starts to brown. Add the onion and habanero and sauté until the onion is soft.

Add the rice to the mixture and continue to sauté until the rice turns light brown.

In a separate pot, bring the coconut milk and chicken stock to a boil, add the rice mixture, reduce the heat, and simmer, covered, until the rice is done, about 25 to 30 minutes. Serve the rice garnished with the minced cilantro.

Yield: 4 to 6 servings

Heat Scale: Hot

Arroz con Coco y Pasas
(Colombian Coconut Rice with Raisins)

Rice cooked with coconut milk has a unique flavor and is part of the Spanish-Indian cuisine of Colombia. The Colombians on the coasts prefer rice, just as those in the interior depend on corn and potatoes. As a side dish, this delicious rice can be served with grilled meats or fish.

2	cups shredded coconut	½	habanero chile, seeds and stem removed, minced, or substitute 1½ jalapeños
4	cups water		
½	teaspoon salt		
2	tablespoons butter	1	tablespoon butter
1	teaspoon sugar	¼	cup finely chopped onion
½	cup seedless raisins	1½ cups rice	

Soak the coconut in the water for at least 3 hours. Drain the coconut milk through a colander into a bowl, squeezing as much juice out as possible. Reserve the coconut milk and discard the meat.

Pour 3 cups of the liquid, salt, 2 tablespoons butter, sugar, raisins, and habanero into a saucepan. Bring the mixture to a boil and then adjust the heat to a simmer and simmer gently for 3 minutes.

Melt 1 tablespoon butter in a small skillet and sauté the onion until it is soft. Add the onion to the simmering mixture and stir in the rice. Cook this mixture, covered, for 20 to 25 minutes and stir once or twice to check for sticking. If the mixture starts to stick, add some of the remaining coconut liquid and stir thoroughly.

Note: This recipe requires advance preparation.

Yield: 6 servings
Heat Scale: Medium

The Spaniards Didn't Get It

"The association of corn kernels with the globe of the sun and gardens of gold was natural to a people who called gold 'the sun's sweat.' And yet, while they honored gold, they were unable to understand the Spaniard's visceral hunger for it. An old drawing shows an Inca handing a bowl of gold nuggets to a Spaniard and asking, 'Do you eat this gold?' The Spaniard answers, 'We eat this gold.' " —Betty Fussell

Gallo Pinto

(Costa Rican Beans and Rice)

Gallo pinto can be called the national dish of Costa Rica, and it is served at breakfast, lunch, and dinner. As with any dish this popular, everyone has his own version. David Tucker, owner of the Hotel La Mariposa in Quepos, was kind enough to share this recipe with us. Cooks are invited to spice up *gallo pinto* by simply adding some chile powder or more hot sauce to the recipe.

1 cup black beans	½ cup chopped onion
Water	⅓ cup chopped red bell pepper
1 bay leaf	1 tablespoon Worcestershire
4 tablespoons vegetable oil	sauce
¼ teaspoon ground cumin, or to taste	1 teaspoon Lea & Perrins steak sauce
¼ teaspoon dried oregano, or to taste	Tabasco or other Louisiana hot sauce, to taste
1 clove garlic	1½ cups cooked rice
Pinch curry powder	
Salt and freshly ground black pepper to taste	

In a large pot, cover the beans with water and soak for at least 4 hours. Bring the water to a boil. Add the bay leaf, 3 tablespoons of the oil, cumin, oregano, garlic, and curry powder. Reduce the heat and simmer for an hour or until the beans are soft. Season with salt and pepper. Drain the beans and reserve the liquid.

In a large skillet, sauté the onion and pepper in the remaining oil until soft. Add the remaining ingredients.

Combine the beans with the rice mixture. If the mixture is too stiff, add a little of the bean water or chicken stock to achieve the desired consistency.

Note: This recipe requires advance preparation.

Variation: Gallo pinto on the Caribbean side of the country is flavored with local coconuts. Cook the beans in coconut milk with a couple of small hot fresh chiles until the beans are soft. Drain and add sautéed onion and garlic. Combine with cooked rice, garnish with chopped cilantro, and serve.

Yield: 4 servings

Heat Scale: Varies, but usually mild

Frijoles Negros

(Brazilian Black Beans)

Corn and potatoes have been staples in the diet of many Latin countries, and beans also rank high on the staple list because of their high protein content. Many of the poorer people eat very little meat, but their diets include a variety of beans. In Brazil, the black bean is so favored that the national dish is called Feijoada Completa (p. 90), and it centers on black beans. This dish is also popular in Colombia and Venezuela. Serve the beans with cooked rice.

1	pound dried black beans, rinsed	3	tablespoons vegetable oil
8	cups hot water	1	cup chopped onion
6	cups hot water	2	cloves garlic, minced
1	habanero chile, left whole, or substitute 3 jalapeños		Salt and freshly ground black pepper
			Cooked white rice

Place the cleaned beans in a heavy Dutch oven or casserole and cover them with 8 cups of hot water. Bring the beans to a boil, then boil for 2 minutes, uncovered. Remove the pot from the heat, cover, and set aside to soak for 1 hour.

Drain the soaked beans. While the beans are draining, clean out the casserole pot and return the beans to the clean pot and cover with the 6 cups of hot water. Add the whole habanero. Bring the beans to a boil, lower the heat to a simmer, cover, and simmer for an hour, or until the beans are tender. Remove the habanero. Using a colander, remove about one-third of the beans from the pot, draining the cooking liquid back into the pot. Set aside.

Heat the oil in a large skillet and sauté the onion for 30 seconds. Add the garlic and toss for a few seconds in the onion-oil mixture. Add the drained beans and mash them with a potato masher until the beans are smooth. Return this mixture to the pot of cooked beans and stir thoroughly. Reheat for 20 minutes, or until the beans are hot and bubbling. Add salt and pepper to taste. Serve the beans with hot rice.

Yield: 6 to 8 servings

Heat Scale: Mild

Potatoes as Panacea

"Slices of raw potatoes, treated with salt or vinegar, were (and are) pasted on the temples to cure headaches. Rubbing healing wounds with *chuñu* flour, powdered brick and vinegar, would prevent scars. If potato was ground up with willow ash and olive oil, it was supposed to prevent rabies. Because potatoes are good retainers of heat, they were supposed to alleviate gout, cure rash, pimples, erysipelas and other skin disorders. A cold poultice applied to burns prevented blisters."

—Carleton Beals

Frijoles Negros en Salsa de Nueces

(Black Beans in Walnut Sauce)

This recipe is an elegant variation of simply cooked black beans. It is from Peru, and, true to tradition, it is hot and spicy with the addition of rocoto or ají chiles. When sautéeing the garlic, be very careful not to burn it, or it will give an "off" taste to this dish.

1 pound black beans, boiled according to the Brazilian Black Beans recipe (p. 218) and pressed through a sieve to eliminate the skins	4 rocoto chiles, seeds and stems removed, minced, or substitute jalapeños
¼ pound bacon, cut into ¼-inch pieces	¼ teaspoon salt
3 tablespoons bacon fat	¼ teaspoon freshly ground black pepper
3 cloves garlic, mashed	¾ cup evaporated milk or half-and-half
1 cup chopped onions	3 hard-boiled eggs, thinly sliced for garnish
¾ cup coarsely chopped walnuts	

In a small skillet, fry the bacon until it is crisp. Drain the bacon and reserve the fat.

Add the garlic and the onions and sauté until the onions are soft. Then add the walnuts, chiles, salt, pepper, and bean puree, and mix well, adding the milk a little at a time until the beans are creamy.

Pour the mixture into an ovenproof dish and bake at 350°F for 15 to 20 minutes.

Garnish with the reserved cooked bacon and the egg slices.

Yield: 6 to 8 servings

Heat Scale: Hot

Camotes Fritos

(Hot Fried Sweet Potatoes)

Another mainstay of South American cooking is the sweet potato, which comes in several varieties, and some of these relatives can be found in Hispanic markets in the United States. In fact, a variation of this Brazilian recipe, sweet potato chips, accompanied a sandwich that we had in a bistro here in Albuquerque.

Vegetable oil for frying

3 sweet potatoes, peeled and cut lengthwise into strips, slightly thicker than ¼-inch

Salt to taste

Habanero powder to taste, or substitute piquin or cayenne

Heat the oil in a fryer or in a deep saucepan and when a drop of water bounces on the oil, add a few of the strips and fry them until they are lightly browned, about 2 to 3 minutes. Drain the strips on paper towels, salt lightly, and dust with the chile powder. Repeat this process with the remaining strips, adjusting the frying time if it's necessary. Keep the fries hot in the oven.

Variation: After draining the strips, refry them for extra crispness before spicing them.

Yield: 4 to 6 servings

Heat Scale: Varies

Llapingachos
(Ecuadorian Spiced Potato Cakes)

Our friend, Loretta Salazar, who lived in Ecuador for several years, collected this recipe. The Llapingachos can accompany other entrees, or can be served as an entree when accompanied by a salad of lettuce, tomatoes, and avocado slices. Sometimes, each potato cake is topped with a fried egg or accompanied with a hot sauce from Chapter 2.

4 cups diced, peeled raw potatoes	½ cup small-curd, low-fat cottage cheese
½ teaspoon salt	
1 egg yolk	¼ cup chopped fresh ají chiles, or substitute yellow wax hot chiles or jalapeños
2 tablespoons cornstarch	
1½ cups chopped onion	
2 tablespoons margarine	¼ cup vegetable oil
½ cup freshly grated Parmesan cheese	

Place the potatoes in a large saucepan, cover with water, and add the salt. Bring to a boil and cook until tender, about 10 to 15 minutes. Drain and mash. Add the egg yolk and cornstarch and mix well. Set aside.

Sauté the onions in the margarine until golden. Add the cheeses and the chile and mix well.

Shape the mashed potato mixture into 10 balls, putting some of the cheese-chile mixture in the center of each. Refrigerate for 30 minutes.

Flatten the balls slightly and sauté in the hot oil until well browned on both sides.

Yield: 5 to 6 servings

Heat Scale: Medium to Hot

Papas Arequipeña

(Fiery Potatoes in Peanut and Cheese Sauce)

Here is yet another Peruvian sauce for potatoes. The city of Arequipa is renowned for its fondness for very hot and spicy foods, so the addition of rocoto chiles in this recipe is a natural. The potatoes may be served as a vegetarian entree or as a separate course.

¾ cup salted, roasted peanuts
½ to ¾ cup half-and-half
     Salt and freshly ground black
     pepper to taste
2   to 3 fresh rocoto chiles, seeds
     and stems removed, or substi-
     tute jalapeños
½ cup grated Monterey Jack
     cheese, or substitute Muenster

3   scallions, including some of the
     green
6   medium boiling potatoes,
     peeled
6   Bibb (Boston) lettuce leaves
6   hard-boiled eggs, halved
     lengthwise
12 ripe olives, halved lengthwise
     Cilantro for garnish

In a blender, puree the peanuts, ½ cup half-and-half, salt, pepper, chiles, cheese, and the scallions. The mixture should resemble mayonnaise. If the mixture seems too thick, add more half-and-half, a little at a time.

Boil the potatoes until they can be pierced with the tip of a sharp knife. Do not overcook. Drain the potatoes, cool slightly, and then cut them in half lengthwise.

On each of six individual plates, put a lettuce leaf, 2 halves of the potato (cut side down), drizzle with the sauce, and garnish with the hard-boiled egg, olives, and cilantro.

Yield: 6 servings

Heat Scale: Medium

Papas Huancaino Numero Uno

(Potatoes Huancayo-Style)

This dish is one version of a popular, traditional potato dish from the high-lands of Peru. Many recipes call for a local herb, *palillo*, which colors the dish a bright yellow; however, turmeric can be substituted. As *Chile Pepper* writer Mary Dempsey pointed out, it is "originally from the Andes mountain town of Huancayo—the final stop on the world's highest single-gauge rail line. It is one of Peru's most popular plates and can be found throughout the country." This dish is typically served with small pieces of corn on the cob.

Juice of 1 small lemon
1 teaspoon ají chile powder, or substitute New Mexican
½ teaspoon salt
¼ teaspoon freshly ground black pepper
1 medium onion, thinly sliced and separated into rings
1½ cups grated Monterey Jack or Muenster cheese
2 fresh rocoto chiles, halved, seeds and stems removed, or substitute yellow wax hot chiles or jalapeños

½ teaspoon turmeric
1 to 1½ cups half-and-half
⅓ cup olive oil
8 Bibb (Boston) lettuce leaves
8 medium potatoes, boiled, peeled, and halved lengthwise
4 hard-boiled eggs, halved lengthwise
2 to 3 ears cooked corn on the cob, cut into 8 2-inch rounds
½ cup sliced black olives

In a ceramic bowl, combine the lemon juice, ground chile, salt, black pepper, and the onion slices. Allow to marinate at room temperature for 1 to 2 hours.

In a blender, puree the cheese, fresh chiles, turmeric, and the cream. If the mixture seems too thick, add more cream, a little at a time.

Heat the oil in a skillet. Pour in the cheese-cream mixture and reduce the heat to very low. Cook for a few minutes, stirring constantly until the sauce is smooth, and thick and creamy.

Arrange the lettuce leaves on a platter or on individual plates. Top the leaves with the potatoes, cut side down, and pour the sauce over the potatoes. Garnish the platter or plates with the eggs, corn slices, and the olives.

Drain the onion rings and absorb any excess with paper towels. Arrange the onion rings over the potatoes.

Yield: 8 servings

Heat Scale: Medium

The Potato—A Chilean Legend

"A chief on Chiloé Island, a place populated by seagulls, wanted to make love like the gods. When pairs of gods embraced, the earth shook and tidal waves were set moving. That much was known, but no one had seen them. Anxious to surprise them, the chief swam out to the forbidden isle. All he got to see was a giant lizard, with its mouth wide open and full of foam and an outside tongue that gave off fire at the tip. The gods buried the indiscreet chief in the ground and condemned him to be eaten by the others. As punishment for his curiosity, they covered his body with blind eyes."

—Eduardo Galeano

Papas Huancaino Numero Dos
(Potatoes Huancayo-Style)

This version of spicy Peruvian potatoes calls for cream cheese and cottage cheese instead of the *queso blanco* in the previous recipe. It also calls for ajís instead of rocotos, but that won't make much difference unless you grow your own, as we do in our Albuquerque garden.

8   ounces cream cheese
12 ounces small-curd cottage cheese
½ to ¾ cup half-and-half
¼ to ½ cup olive oil
¾ teaspoon turmeric
2   cloves garlic, minced
½ cup minced onion
3   fresh ají chiles, seeds and stems removed, finely minced, or substitute yellow wax hot chiles or jalapeños

12 black olives, coarsely chopped
1   head lettuce, shredded
8   large potatoes, cooked, cooled, and quartered
3   hard-boiled eggs, sliced
    Garnish: ¼ cup diced green and red sweet peppers; 4 sprigs cilantro or parsley, chopped; 2 boiled eggs, sliced; 8 black olives

In a large mixing bowl, combine the cheeses and beat with a hand mixer until they are well blended. Gradually add the half-and-half and the oil, beating continuously. Then add the *palillo* or turmeric, garlic, onion, and the chiles and beat thoroughly, adding more cream if the mixture seems too thick to be pourable. Stir in the chopped black olives.

Arrange the shredded lettuce on a platter, arrange the potatoes on top, and cover with the sauce. Garnish with the hard-boiled eggs and the remaining garnishes. Serve at room temperature.

Yield: 6 to 8 servings
Heat Scale: Medium

The Invention of Freeze-Drying

"Archaeology has also revealed prehistoric stories of *chuño* or dehydrated potato. The method for making this seems to have remained unchanged right up to the present, and this product is of great importance to the South American Indians, as it forms the major item in their winter stores. To make it, they expose the potatoes by night to severe frost, then trample them to extract the juice and expose them to the sun and dry air throughout the day. The process lasts for four or five days."

—Don and Patricia Brothwell

Ensalada con Quinoa de Peru
(Peruvian Quinoa Salad)

Quinoa is a very versatile grain. It can be added to soups, stews, and salads for additional nutrition and texture. It was a staple of the Incas, who called it "the mother grain." Quinoa was cultivated on the terraces of Machu Picchu, as it successfully grows at high altitudes. Today, it is still an important food in Peru, Bolivia, and Ecuador. Its flavor has been compared to couscous or wild rice. In the United States, it is commonly available in natural food supermarkets and health food stores in several forms: the whole grain, flour, and pasta. Some nutritionists call it a complete protein because it contains all eight essential amino acids.

2 cups raw quinoa	8 scallions, the white part thinly sliced
8½ cups water	⅓ cup minced Italian parsley
⅓ cup fresh lime juice	⅓ cup minced fresh mint
2 fresh ají chiles, seeds and stems removed, finely chopped, or substitute yellow wax hot chiles, jalapeños, or serranos	Salt and freshly ground black pepper to taste
⅔ cup olive oil	Garnishes: 2 heads Bibb lettuce, shredded; 3 hard-boiled eggs, thinly sliced; 2 fresh ears of corn, cooked and cut into 2-inch rounds; 1 cup black olives, thickly sliced
2 medium cucumbers, peeled, seeded, and cubed into ½-inch pieces	
1 large ripe tomato, seeded and cubed	

Prepare the quinoa by rinsing it thoroughly under cold running water. Keep rinsing until the water runs clear. Combine the quinoa with 8½ cups of cold water in a heavy saucepan. Bring the quinoa to a boil, then reduce the heat to a simmer and cook for 10 minutes, or until all the grains are translucent. Drain and transfer the quinoa to a large bowl and chill.

In a small bowl, whisk together the lime juice, chiles, and olive oil and set aside.

When the quinoa is cool, add the cucumbers, tomato, scallions, parsley, and mint and mix gently. Pour the lime juice mixture over the top of the quinoa-vegetable mixture and toss again. Add the salt and freshly ground black pepper to taste.

To serve the salad, place a mound of shredded Bibb lettuce on 6 or 8 individual plates and garnish with any or all of the suggested garnishes.

Yield: 6 to 8 servings

Heat Scale: Medium

Keen on Quinoa

"Quinoa's large seedheads and broad leaves make it look something like a cross between sorghum and spinach. Its grain is rich in protein and contains a better amino balance than the protein in most of the true cereals. In earlier times this grain helped sustain the awesome Incan armies as they marched throughout the empire on new conquests. Today, it is made into flour for baked goods, breakfast cereals, beer, soups, desserts, and even livestock feed." —*Lost Crops of the Incas*

Ensalada con Quinoa de Bolivia

(Bolivian Quinoa Salad)

Considered a miracle grain, quinoa once again shows its versatility. It becomes almost transparent when it is cooked, and its taste is mild and blends very well with any number of ingredients. Quinoa was a staple of the Incas who thought it was so important that it was sacred. It was a much overlooked grain in the United States until recently, when its nutritional value increased the demand for it.

1 cup quinoa	⅓ cup chopped walnuts
4 cups water	¼ cup raisins
½ cup chopped red bell pepper	¼ teaspoon salt
2 cloves garlic, minced	¼ teaspoon freshly ground black pepper
1 cup chopped onions	⅓ cup olive oil
½ cup chopped celery	2 tablespoons fresh lime juice
1 fresh ají chile, seeds and stem removed, chopped fine, or substitute yellow wax hot chile or jalapeño	1 tablespoon white wine vinegar

Wash the quinoa thoroughly, until the water runs clear. Place the quinoa in a large saucepan, add the water, and bring to a boil. Reduce the heat and simmer for 10 minutes or until the quinoa is tender. Drain the quinoa and place it in a large bowl and chill.

When the quinoa is chilled, add the remaining ingredients, except the oil, lime juice, and vinegar, and mix thoroughly.

In a small jar, mix the olive oil, lime juice, and vinegar, and shake. Drizzle the dressing over the salad and toss.

Yield: 4 servings

Heat Scale: Mild

Imagine What They Thought About Chiles

"Within twenty years [of their discovery by Europeans] white potatoes were sold in Spanish markets, but they were far less popular than the sweet potato. Sir Walter Raleigh planted white potatoes on his estate in Ireland and they quickly filled an important food need for the Irish people, but across the Irish Sea in England only Elizabeth and those of her court were familiar with the tuber. In Scotland the potato was slow to gain acceptance, too, because certain Presbyterian clergy declared the vegetable had not been mentioned in the Bible and therefore was not safe to eat." —Betty Wasson

Humitas con Achiote

(Pureed Corn with Annatto)

This dish is especially popular in Argentina and Chile, but it is served throughout South America, with each cook or chef adding his or her particular trademark. The best versions are made from very young corn, although frozen corn kernels are a good substitute. These *humitas* are wrapped in dried corn husks and steamed like tamales. They can be served as a snack or as an accompaniment for meat or chicken dishes.

2 dried ají chiles, seeds and stems removed, soaked in hot water for 20 minutes, or substitute ancho, pasilla, or New Mexican	½ teaspoon salt
4 cups fresh young corn kernels, or substitute 4 cups defrosted frozen corn kernels	4 tablespoons achiote oil (p. 15), or substitute 2 tablespoons butter, 2 tablespoons olive oil and ½ teaspoon paprika
⅓ cup milk	¾ cup minced onion
2 eggs	1 clove garlic, minced
¼ teaspoon freshly ground black pepper	¼ cup grated Parmesan cheese
	20–22 dried corn husks
	String for tying

Combine the chiles, corn, and milk in a blender and puree on high for 20 seconds. Add the eggs, black pepper, and salt, and blend for 15 more seconds, or until the mixture is thick.

Heat the achiote oil in a large, heavy skillet. When the oil is hot, add the onions and sauté over medium heat until they are almost soft, then add the garlic and sauté for 30 seconds, taking care that the garlic does not burn.

Pour the pureed corn mixture into the frying pan and reduce the heat to low. Simmer, uncovered, for 5 to 7 minutes, stirring frequently until the mixture thickens. Stir in the grated cheese and keep stirring until the cheese melts, then remove the skillet from the heat.

Place 2 tablespoons of the seasoned corn in each corn husk and roll the husk around the mixture, tucking in the ends.

Tie each individual husk with the string.

Stack the husks on a rack and steam in a large pot for 2 hours.

Yield: 20 to 22 husks

Heat Scale: Mild

Latin Onion Names

"Latin Americans know their onions and have separate names for the many different kinds—*cebolla,* ordinary onion; *cebolleta,* a tender onion; *cebollino,* a young onion; *cebollón,* a large onion; and last, as well as least in size, *cebollitas,* tiny pickled onions that certainly have piquance." —Cora, Rose, and Bob Brown

Guiso de Repollo

(Bolivian Cabbage in Tomato Sauce)

Cabbage dishes are found all over Latin America, probably because cabbage is so easy to grow and is such a versatile vegetable that can be served cooked, raw in salads (such as coleslaw), or as sauerkraut. The latter dish shows the European influence in Latin America. Generally, green, white, and red varieties of cabbage are available.

Water
½ teaspoon salt
1 small cabbage, white or green, finely shredded
2 tablespoons olive oil
1 cup chopped onion
2 medium tomatoes, peeled and chopped
2 fresh rocoto chiles, seeds and stems removed, chopped, or substitute jalapeños

¼ teaspoon salt
¼ teaspoon freshly ground black pepper
3 tablespoons chopped cilantro
4 medium potatoes, cooked, peeled, and quartered

Bring a large pot of water to a boil, add the ½ teaspoon salt and the cabbage, and simmer for 4 to 5 minutes. Drain thoroughly and set aside.

Heat the oil in a large skillet and sauté the onion until it is soft. Add the tomatoes, chile, salt, pepper, and cilantro and simmer for 1 minute, until the mixture is well blended.

Add the drained cabbage and the potatoes and heat thoroughly.

Yield: 4 servings

Heat Scale: Medium

Repôlho com Vinho
(Chile-Spiced Cabbage with Wine)

This dish is the Brazilian version of Guiso de Repollo (p. 234) from Bolivia. We suggest serving it with grilled or fried meat to add a crunch to the meal. Another interesting addition would be Llapingachos (p. 222) or Camotes Fritos (p. 221).

Water

½ teaspoon salt

1 small green cabbage, finely shredded

2 tablespoons olive oil

1 cup diced onion

1 fresh habanero chile, seeds and stem removed, minced, or substitute 3 jalapeños

1 bell pepper, seeded and chopped

2 tablespoons chopped cilantro

2 tomatoes, peeled, seeded, and chopped

½ cup dry white wine

Bring a large pot of water to a boil, add the salt, and then add the cabbage. Bring the water back to a boil and then simmer the cabbage for 3 to 4 minutes. Drain the cabbage and set aside.

Heat the oil in a large skillet and sauté the onion, peppers, cilantro, and the tomatoes until the onion is soft.

Add the drained cabbage to the skillet and pour the wine over the top. Cover the skillet and simmer the mixture 4 to 5 minutes until it is hot.

Yield: 4 servings

Heat Scale: Medium

Paltas Rellenas

(Peruvian Stuffed Avocados)

Peruvian yellow potatoes are preferred for this recipe. The use of white potatoes will change the color and the taste, but it will still be good. The potato is king in Peru, as it can grow at altitudes where maize won't. Food scholars think that the potato has been grown in the Andean region for 8,000 years; the first Europeans to see the potato were probably Pizarro and his men. A few of the 200 or so relatives of the Andean potato are beginning to show up in North American markets, but they are grown by local farmers.

1	pound yellow potatoes, cooked, peeled, and pressed through a fine sieve	3	large, ripe avocados
1	rocoto chile, seeds and stem removed, ground or finely grated, or substitute jalapeño	2	ears fresh corn, cooked and cut into rounds
3	tablespoons grated onion	12	prawns or shrimp, cooked, peeled, and deveined, drizzled with olive oil, and sprinkled with red chile powder
1	tablespoon fresh lime juice	12	black olives
3	to 5 tablespoons olive oil Bibb lettuce leaves		Salt and freshly ground black pepper to taste

Mix the sieved potatoes with the rocoto chile, onion, lime juice, and add enough olive oil to make a thick puree.

Arrange the lettuce leaves on 3 plates.

Cut the avocados in half, discard the seed, and place 2 halves on each plate. Stuff them with the potato mixture.

Garnish each plate with the corn, shrimp, and olives, and season with salt and pepper.

Yield: 3 servings

Heat Scale: Mild

Picante de Aguacates

(Spicy Chilean Avocados)

The Aztec name for avocado translates into "testicle tree," referring to their shape and the fact that they grow in pairs. The avocado made its way south into Peru, Ecuador, and Chile and was in Peru at the time Pizarro arrived. This spicy, stuffed avocado is a good side dish for grilled meat or some of that fine Chilean fish.

3	hard-boiled egg yolks	3	tablespoons chopped cilantro
2	fresh ají chiles, seeds and stems removed, minced, or substitute yellow wax hot chiles or jalapeños	3	tablespoons champagne vinegar
		½	teaspoon salt
1	clove garlic, minced	¼	teaspoon freshly ground black pepper
1	cup chopped onion	6	large, ripe avocados

Mash the egg yolks and add the remaining ingredients, except the avocados, and mix thoroughly.

Peel 2 of the avocados, discard the seeds, and chop them coarsely. Add them to the egg yolk mixture and mix in gently.

Peel the remaining 4 avocados, discard the seeds, and halve the avocados. Mound the stuffing into the 8 avocado halves.

Yield: 8 servings as a side dish

Heat Scale: Medium

Hongos con Chile y Queso

(Mushrooms with Chile and Cheese)

This is a rich and satisfying side dish from Chile. We suggest serving it with grilled or braised chicken, fish, or meat. The mushrooms can be wild, or use the button variety found in grocery stores.

2 tablespoons butter	2 fresh ají chiles, seeds and stems removed, minced, or substitute yellow wax hot chiles or jalapeños
4 scallions, chopped	
1 clove garlic, minced	
1 pound mushrooms, cleaned and sliced	1 tablespoon fresh cilantro, minced
2 fresh tomatoes, peeled, seeded, and diced	½ cup shredded Muenster or cheddar cheese

Melt the butter in a medium skillet and sauté the scallions and the garlic for 1 minute; add the mushrooms, and toss them in the skillet to coat with the sautéed mixture. Sauté the mixture for a minute or two. Add the tomatoes and the chiles and stir into the mushrooms. Simmer, covered, for 5 minutes.

Drain off any excess liquid from the sautéed mixture and add the cilantro and cheese. Simmer only until the cheese melts.

Yield: 4 to 6 servings as a side dish

Heat Scale: Medium

Habas con Ajís

(Lima Beans with Ají Chiles)

Lima beans were possibly one of the first crops cultivated by Indian farmers; limas were found in excavations dated 5000–6000 B.C. in the coastal regions. The many varieties of limas include the very tiny, or baby limas, to some that are 1½-inches long. This easy and delicious Peruvian recipe is a good side dish for any of the meat recipes because its flavor is not overwhelming, and it will complement any dish.

2	tablespoons butter
1	tablespoon olive oil
1	leek, white part only, finely diced
2	fresh ají chiles, seeds and stems removed, minced, or substitute yellow wax hot chiles or jalapeños
16	ounces (about 4 cups) fresh lima beans, or 1 package frozen baby lima beans, thawed (Do not use dried beans.)

½	to 1 cup water
1	tablespoon fresh lemon or lime juice
1	teaspoon lemon or lime zest
¼	teaspoon salt
¼	teaspoon freshly ground black pepper

Melt 1 tablespoon of the butter with the olive oil in a small, heavy skillet. Add the leek and ají chiles and sauté for 30 seconds. Add the lima beans, water, and the citrus juice; bring the mixture to a boil, and then lower the heat to a simmer, cover and simmer for 8 to 10 minutes.

Mix the 1 remaining tablespoon of butter with the citrus zest and the salt and pepper. When the beans are tender, drain them, and add the butter mixture. Simmer for a minute and stir to coat the beans.

Yield: 3 to 4 servings

Heat Scale: Medium

Chayote con Ajís

(Chayote Squash Sautéed with Ají Chiles)

Chayote comes under the guise of many names: chocho and christophene, to name two. It is a squash common to many countries in Latin America, and variations of this recipe appear from Brazil to Chile. It is a versatile vegetable, and it can be stuffed, sautéed, or baked as well as added to soups and stews. We think it has many of the same uses as the zucchini does in the United States.

3	chayote squash, peeled and cubed	2	fresh ají chiles, seeds and stems removed, minced, or substitute yellow wax hot chiles or jalapeños
	Water for boiling		
½	teaspoon salt	1½	cups fresh or frozen corn
2	tablespoons olive oil	1	tablespoon minced cilantro
1	cup chopped onion	¼	cup grated Parmesan cheese
2	cloves garlic, minced		

Boil the cubed chayotes in the salted water for 5 minutes, or until barely done. Drain the squash in a sieve and reserve.

Heat the olive oil in a large skillet and sauté the onion, garlic, and chile until the onion wilts.

Add the chayote to the skillet, along with the corn, and sauté for a minute or two, tossing the ingredients to coat the squash.

Sprinkle the sautéed mixture with the cilantro and the cheese and heat just until the cheese starts to melt and coat the mixture. Serve immediately.

Yield: 6 to 8 servings

Heat Scale: Medium

9

Bien Me Sabe
Cool-Down Drinks and Desserts

One of the earliest drinks of Latin America was *chicha*, a fermented beer-like beverage made from maize that was a favorite of the Incas. The chronicler Bernabe Cobo wrote extensively on the subject and noted that it was socially correct for Incan royalty to bring along a jug of *chicha* when they visited friends. Drunkenness, although common, drew stiff punishments. The first offense was punished by the judge as he saw fit; the second offense drew exile, and on a third inebriated occasion the offender was sent to work in the mines.

Another famous Latin American drink that is enormously popular is *yerba maté*, a tea made from a species of holly. Because of immigrants from Italy, Portugal, Spain, and France, the wines of Argentina and Chile are particularly renowned.

For our drink selections, first we offer two *batidas*, or blended beverages. The Batida de Bahia (Brazilian Tropical Fruit Drink, p. 244) features pineapple, banana, and optional rum, while the Batida de Leite (Brazilian Milk Punch, p. 245) has both cow's milk and coconut milk. Two holiday drinks follow. Ponche

241

de Piña (Spicy Pineapple Punch, p. 246) is from Central America and is served hot on festive occasions. Rompope (Ecuadorian Eggnog, p. 247) is a delightful cocktail.

Many Latin drinks feature citrus. Our Pisco Agrio (Pisco Sour, p. 248) spotlights the famous Pisco brandy that is so popular in Peru and other Andean countries. Caipirinha (Peasant's Drink, p. 249) is far from plebian, as it features limes blended with the fine Brazilian rum *cachaça*. That rum is also combined with coconut in Cachaça de Coco (Coconut Rum, p. 250). Another rum drink is Rum y Agua de Coco (Rum and Coconut Water, p. 251), which is popular throughout South America.

Coffee, of course, is grown in many Latin countries—particularly Brazil, Colombia, and Guatemala. It is so popular in Brazil that Cora, Rose, and Bob Brown write of some coffee enthusiasts who drink forty cups a day! They also mentioned that it is beloved by the family parrots. Champurrado (Guatemalan Chocolate Coffee, p. 252) combines two beloved ingredients into a tasty after dinner drink.

Coconuts and tropical fruits play a large role in Latin desserts. Brasileiras (Brazilians, p. 253) are coconut cookies that are extremely popular in Brazil. Los Turrones de Doña Pepe (The Dainties of Doña Pepe, p. 254) are Peruvian pastries flavored with cinnamon and anise. Mezcolanza de Frutas Tropicales (Jumble of Tropical Fruits, p. 255) combines papayas and mangoes with other familiar fruits, although other exotic fruits from the tropics may be substituted as they become more available. Gelado de Abacate (Avocado Ice Cream, p. 256) is unusual yet delicious.

We have collected a medley of four South American custards to show the wide range of flavorings for this Latin favorite. Flan de Coco Peruano (Peruvian Coconut Custard, p. 257) is the simplest of the four, while Pudim de Coco e Abacaxi (Brazilian Coconut-Pineapple Custard, p. 258) adds pineapple for an interesting twist. Bien-Me-Sabe (Tastes Good to Me, p. 259) also translates as "I know it well" and is unusual because it features squash. Qumbolitos (Anise Flavored Cakes in Canna Leaves, p. 260), an Ecuadorian custard, is flavored with raisins and anise. Plantanos con Crema Natilla (Cinnamon-Spiced Plantains with Natilla Cream, p. 261) is an easy dessert that can also be made with bananas.

Tropical fruits are also found in our Latin pies. Torta de Coco com Frutas (Coconut Pie with Tropical Fruits, p. 262) gives the cook a choice of toppings. Almonds and mangoes unite in Pastel de Almendras y Mango

(Almond and Mango Pie, p. 263), while bananas and walnuts do the same in Pastel de Platanos y Nogadas (Banana and Walnut Pie, p. 264), a Venezuelan dessert.

A quartet of cakes concludes this chapter. Bolo de Nozes com Vinho (Brazil Nut Wine Cake, p. 265) features one of the few crops still collected in the wild rather than cultivated—Brazil nuts. Tortas de Cacao (Colombian Cocoa Cakes, p. 266) are simple and delicious, and Torta Criolla de Queso (Creole Passion Fruit Cheesecake, p. 267) is more elaborate but well worth the trouble. Raisins take center stage in Torta de Pasa (Raisin Cake, p. 268), from Paraguay.

The Chocolate Monopoly

"Around 1600, with the introduction of cocoa cultivation, the structure of the Venezuelan economy was established for the next 300 years. In the Caracas of 1684 wealth was amazingly concentrated: 172 people held a total of 167 cocoa plantations with 450,000 trees. By the 1740s, cocoa production in the province of Caracas had multiplied tenfold, but the number of cocoa proprietors had increased by only 3. The church controlled about a fifth of the cocoa area in the 1740s, but even this was less than the area owned by a single family, the Pontes." —Chantal Coady

Batida de Bahia

(Brazilian Tropical Fruit Drink)

In Brazil, a *batida* is any kind of drink, alcoholic or not, which is mixed in an electric blender. Feel free to use any kind of fruit, especially the tropical ones that are becoming more popular. Experiment with Latin American fruits such as passion fruit, papayas (Solo variety preferred), sapodilla, and the juice of rambutans, which are native to Southeast Asia but are now found in Central American countries such as Costa Rica.

1½	cups pineapple juice		Juice of ½ lime
1	ripe banana, cut up	¼	cup rum (optional)
4	red maraschino cherries	1	cup crushed ice
1	tablespoon honey	4	sprigs fresh mint

Place the pineapple juice in a blender and turn on high speed. Drop in the remaining ingredients except the mint and blend for 30 seconds. Serve in cocktail glasses and garnish with the mint.

Yield: 4 servings

Batida de Leite
(Brazilian Milk Punch)

Another version of the Brazilian *batida* calls for cow's milk along with the fruits. This is a typical drink from Rio; feel free to substitute papaya for the mango.

1   cup canned coconut milk (not sweetened coconut syrup)

1   cup cow's milk

¾   cup mashed ripe mango

¼   cup lime juice

¼   cup *cachaça* or light rum (optional)

1   cup crushed ice

Place all ingredients in a blender, turn on high speed and blend for about 30 seconds.

Yield: 3 servings

The Incas Party Down

The beverage of choice among the Incas was *chicha,* a beer made from maize. According to one historian, "Drunkenness and intemperance in drinking was a passion with this people, the source of all their ills, and even their idolatry. The days of triumph for victories won, the days of plowing the earth, the days of planting of the maize, it was open to everybody to drink as much as they wanted."

Ponche de Piña

(Spicy Pineapple Punch)

This hot pineapple punch is popular in Honduras and Nicaragua, especially around Christmas. The rum is optional but always seems to crop up in Latin American drinks.

3	fresh pineapples, peeled, cored, and shredded	1	2-inch stick cinnamon
	Water	1	tablespoon brown sugar
2	teaspoons whole cloves	1	cup coconut milk (not sweetened coconut syrup)
2	teaspoons whole allspice (*pimento*)	½	cup light rum

Place the pineapple in a bowl, add water to cover and let stand overnight in the refrigerator.

Combine the pineapple in a large pot with the remaining ingredients except the rum. Bring to a boil and boil for 5 minutes, stirring constantly. Remove from the heat, strain, add the rum, and serve in mugs.

Note: This recipe requires advance preparation.

Yield: 8 servings

Rompope

(Ecuadorian Eggnog)

Whether you're in Ecuador or New England, on holiday evenings there's no better starter than a special eggnog cocktail. Of course, in Ecuador, this would be made with Pisco brandy.

1 quart milk	1 teaspoon vanilla
1 cup sugar	Pisco brandy, cognac, or rum to taste
3 sticks cinnamon	
⅛ teaspoon ground anise	Nutmeg to taste
6 egg yolks, well beaten	

Boil the milk with the sugar, cinnamon, and anise until it reduces a little. Remove from the stove and cool. Add the egg yolks a little at a time, stirring constantly. Continuing to stir, heat slowly to the boiling point. Remove from the stove and strain.

When cool, add the vanilla and brandy, cognac, or rum to taste. Place the eggnog in a bottle, cover, and place in the refrigerator until needed. Serve in cocktail or champagne glasses and sprinkle with nutmeg.

Yield: 8 to 10 cocktails

Pisco Agrio

(Pisco Sour)

Here is the famous drink that is so popular in Peru, Bolivia, and Chile. The main ingredient, Pisco, is a brandy distilled from Muscat wine. It is available at better wine and liquor stores.

¼ cup Pisco brandy	¼ teaspoon bitters
1 tablespoon honey	1 egg white
2 tablespoons lemon juice	2 cups crushed ice

In a bowl, mix together the Pisco, honey, lemon juice, and bitters and stir well to dissolve the honey. Transfer to a cocktail shaker, add the egg white and crushed ice, and shake vigorously. Strain into cocktail glasses and serve.

Yield: 4 servings

The *Chicha* Chug-a-Lug

"How much [*chicha*] consumption was 'too much'? For all the rhetoric, few bothered to note specific amounts. Speculative calculations can be made. Potosí used 50,000 *fanegas* of maize flour to produce 1.6 million *botijas* of *chicha* in 1603. With an estimated Indian population of 60,000, of whom perhaps 50 percent regularly drank *chicha,* per capita yearly consumption was 53 *botijas,* or about three gallons per day."

—John C. Super

Caipirinha

(Peasant's Drink)

This is supposedly the national drink of Brazil, named for the Portuguese word *caipira*, meaning peasant. It is best to use Brazilian *cachaça* in this drink, but any powerful white rum will work.

1 lime, quartered	1 cup crushed ice
¼ cup *cachaça*	2 lime quarters for garnish
1½ teaspoons sugar	

Squeeze the 4 lime quarters into a cocktail shaker, add the *cachaca*, sugar, and ice, and shake. Pour into highball glasses and garnish with the 2 lime quarters.

Yield: 2 servings

Nun Wars

"There are many fine modern commercial pastry shops in South America, but traditionally the best *golosinas,* or sweets, are made in and sold by convents, which at one time had a monopoly on producing sweets. This tradition dates back to colonial times and is very much alive today. The convents have always taken great pride in their sweets and competed furiously with one another both to create the finest sweets and to attract customers. It is said that when nuns from different convents would meet and begin to discuss sweets, the discussion sometimes got so heated they would pull one another's headdresses and start hitting each other!"

—Felipe Rojas-Lombardi

Cachaça de Coco
(Coconut Rum)

The raconteur, Charles Baker, wrote about this fascinating recipe in *The South American Gentleman's Companion*. This is not a quick recipe, so be forewarned. Baker noted, "Naturally, the longer you leave it buried the more mellowed it gets."

1   large coconut, not too ripe
     White rum

Drill out one of the "eyes" of the coconut and pour out the coconut water, reserving it for the next recipe. Fill up the coconut with rum, and stopper it with a carved wood stopper lightly pounded into the coconut. Place it in a cool, dark place (Baker said to bury it in the ground) for six months. Unstopper the coconut and pour out the amber liquor.

Yield: Varies according to the size of the coconut

Demon Cachaça

"Colourless sugar cane spirit was drunk all over Brazil as Cachaça (pronounced kachassa), the country's national drink. To John Gunther *(Inside Brazil),* it was 'this sinister but enlivening fluid' with different versions all over South America. It was the drink of the masses, universally available at between 94 and 100 proof, 'the effects of which can be devastating.' Cachaça mixed with mashed lemon slices, sugar, and ice became the national cocktail, *caipirinha.*"

—Hugh Barty-King and Anton Massel

Rum y Agua de Coco

(Rum and Coconut Water)

This combination is popular all over South America and the West Indies. In fact, Dave and Mary Jane were introduced to it in Trinidad, which is right off the coast of Venezuela. Scotch is surprisingly good as a substitute for the rum.

¼ cup white rum

2 teaspoons sugar syrup

Juice of ½ lime

2 cups fresh coconut water

1 cup crushed ice

Soda water

Orange slices for garnish

Combine all ingredients except the soda water in a cocktail shaker. Shake well and pour off into cocktail glasses. Top with a small shot of soda water and garnish with the orange slices.

Yield: 4 to 6 servings

Champurrado

(Guatemalan Chocolate Coffee)

Called a *champurrado* because it is a combination of two different drinks, this traditional chocolate-coffee mixture is a delightful breakfast or dessert drink. This recipe is designed to serve a small party.

4	squares unsweetened chocolate	2	tablespoons ground cinnamon
	Water	1	large piece vanilla bean
1	cup sugar		Pinch salt
2	tablespoons cornstarch	6	cups hot milk
4	cups black coffee		Ground cinnamon for garnish

In a double boiler over low heat, melt the chocolate with a little water. Combine the sugar and cornstarch, add to the chocolate, and mix well. Add the coffee, stir well and heat for 10 minutes. Add the cinnamon, vanilla bean, salt, and milk and cook over medium heat for 35 minutes, stirring occasionally.

Remove the vanilla bean and serve in cups sprinkled with a pinch of ground cinnamon.

Yield: 8 to 10 servings

Brasileiras

(Brazilians)

These coconut cookies are a favorite in Brazil. They are best when made with freshly grated coconut.

1 cup sugar	3 tablespoons plain flour
¾ cup water	3 egg yolks
1½ cups grated fresh coconut	½ teaspoon vanilla
1 tablespoon butter	

Preheat the oven to 350°F.

Combine the sugar and water in a saucepan and boil steadily until the sugar reaches the thread stage, about 232°F. Add the remaining ingredients except the vanilla and reduce the heat. Cook over low heat, stirring constantly, until the mixture does not stick to the side of the pan. Remove from the heat, let cool, and stir in the vanilla.

Drop spoonfuls of the batter onto a greased cookie sheet and bake at 350°F for 15 minutes or until golden brown. Take care not to burn the cookies.

Yield: 3 dozen

Los Turrones de Doña Pepe
(The Dainties of Doña Pepe)

This pastry is prepared during the month of October in Peru for the festivities of "Our Lord of the Miracles." At the end of October, a procession takes place to celebrate the miracle of the Sacred Image on the Wall that survived the devastating 1655 earthquake. During the procession, *Los Turrones de Doña Pepe* are sold by street vendors. No one knows who Doña Pepe was—only her name and her dainties survive, although we've shortened them from their traditional size of 12 inches.

4	cups flour	2	cups water
4	teaspoons baking powder	5	whole cloves
1	teaspoon salt	1	3-inch stick cinnamon
1	cup shortening	1	2- by 2-inch piece orange peel
1	teaspoon anise seed	¼	teaspoon lemon juice
6	tablespoons water	⅛	cup colored decorating sugar
4	egg yolks		
6	cups raw sugar *(chancaca)*, available in Latin markets, or substitute brown sugar		

Sift the flour with the baking powder and salt. Make a well in the mixture and add the shortening, anise seed, water, and egg yolks. Mix with your fingers into a soft dough and roll out into drumsticks 6 inches long and ½-inch in diameter. Place the sticks on a greased baking pan and bake in a 350°F oven for about 20 minutes or until they are golden brown.

Meanwhile, place the raw sugar, water, cloves, cinnamon, and orange peel in a pot and boil it down to a thick syrup. Remove from the heat, and strain. Add the lemon juice, stir, and allow to cool.

Remove the sticks and arrange them on a serving dish in an overlaying vertical and horizontal pattern. Pour the syrup over the *turrones* and sprinkle with the decorating sugar.

Yield: About 20 servings

Mezcolanza de Frutas Tropicales

(Jumble of Tropical Fruits)

We cheerfully admit to inventing this recipe. However, we were inspired by the numerous varieties of tropical fruits now available in North American produce markets, especially the Latin and Asian markets. In Colombia, the fruit would be served in *canastillas*, little baskets made from hollowed-out papayas.

2	mangoes, peeled, pits removed, and chopped	1	cup chopped orange slices
1	small papaya (Solo preferred), peeled, seeds removed, and chopped	3	tablespoons minced fresh mint
		2	cups plain yogurt
2	bananas, peeled and sliced	3	tablespoons sugar
1	cup coarsely chopped pineapple		Whipped cream for garnish
			Ground allspice for garnish

In a large bowl, combine the mangoes, papaya, bananas, pineapple, orange slices, and mint and stir gently.

Place the mixture on 8 individual plates.

Stir together the yogurt and sugar and spoon over the fruit plates. Add a dollop of whipped cream and sprinkle the allspice over the top and serve.

Yield: 8 servings

Gelado de Abacate

(Avocado Ice Cream)

We think of the avocado as a vegetable, but in Brazil it's a fruit, too. This is best when made in an ice-cream maker, but it can also just be frozen in the freezer: its texture is then more like an ice than an ice cream.

6   cups milk
1   cup sugar
1   tablespoon cornstarch
3   eggs
3   ripe avocados, peeled and mashed

Juice of 1 lime
3   tablespoons powdered sugar
1   cup whipping cream

In a saucepan, combine the milk and sugar and heat just to boiling. Dissolve the cornstarch in a little water and add it to the milk and sugar. Boil for 3 minutes, stirring constantly. Remove from the heat and let stand for 5 minutes.

Beat the eggs lightly in a bowl and add the milk mixture, beating constantly. Let cool. Mash the avocados with the lime juice and powdered sugar to make a creamy paste. Add this paste and whipping cream to the egg-milk mixture and stir well. Add to an ice-cream maker and freeze.

Yield: 8 servings

Flan de Coco Peruano

(Peruvian Coconut Custard)

This is an incredibly simple but incredibly tasty dessert that illustrates the Latin love of *flan*. It is quite rich and decadent, so be sure and serve it with a good cognac. You will need 8 custard cups for this recipe, or you can use a shallow-sided oven-proof bowl.

1½ cups sugar (or more if needed)	6 eggs
4 cups shredded fresh coconut	1 teaspoon vanilla
2 cans sweetened condensed milk	

Heat the sugar until it caramelizes, and while thick, pour it into the custard cups. Move the cups around so that the inside of each one is thickly coated.

In a bowl, combine the coconut and the condensed milk. Add the eggs one at a time, beating well. Add the vanilla and stir well. Add the coconut mixture to the caramelized cups and place the cups in a water bath. Bake for 1 to 1½ hours at 350°F, until the custard has just a little bit of a jiggle to it. Take care that the water doesn't evaporate.

Turn the cups or bowl upside down on dessert plates and serve.

Yield: 8 servings

Pudim de Coco e Abacaxi

(Brazilian Coconut-Pineapple Custard)

In Brazil's explosive variation on *flan,* two tropical dessert favorites—coconut and pineapple—are combined in a pudding that's served over a mildly alcoholic sponge cake.

1	15-ounce can condensed milk	⅓	cup rum
1½	cups milk	1	pineapple, peeled, cored, and diced
2	egg yolks, beaten	1	cup freshly grated coconut
3	tablespoons cornstarch	1	cup cream, whipped
½	teaspoon vanilla		Thin slices of mango for garnish
1	9-inch square prepared sponge cake		
1	cup pineapple juice		

In a double boiler, combine the condensed milk, milk, egg yolks, cornstarch, and vanilla. Cook, stirring constantly, over boiling water until the mixture thickens. Cook for 10 more minutes at a simmer without stirring, then remove from the heat and cool.

Cut the sponge cake into 2-inch squares and place in a serving bowl. Combine the pineapple juice and rum and sprinkle the mixture over the sponge cake squares. Cover with one-half of the custard mixture, then one-half of the pineapple, then one-half of the coconut. Cover with the remaining custard mixture and top with whipped cream. Garnish with the remaining coconut, pineapple, and the mango slices.

Yield: 6 servings

Bien-Me-Sabe

(Tastes Good to Me)

Our third custard is Andean and is the most unusual because it's made with *zapallo, Curcurbita maxima,* the Peruvian winter pumpkin or squash. Two reasonable substitutes are Chilean varieties now popular in the United States and Canada: acorn and Hubbard. This custard is considerably thinner than the other two *flans.*

6	pounds winter squash, peeled, seeded, and chopped	2	cups sugar
	Water to cover	10	egg yolks
¼	teaspoon anise seed	¼	cup sweet white wine
3	cups milk		Ground cinnamon for garnish

In a large pot, boil the squash in the water with the anise seed until tender. Drain the squash, run through a sieve, and return to the pot with the milk and sugar. Cook until thick, stirring occasionally.

Beat the egg yolks with the white wine, add to the squash mixture, and cook over low heat until very thick. Remove from the heat and allow to set. Spoon the custard out of the pan, sprinkle with the cinnamon, and serve.

Yield: 8 servings

Qumbolitos

(Anise Flavored Cakes in Canna Leaves)

Our final custard recipe is an Ecuadorian dessert from our friend, Louella Buchanan, who lived in Quito for many years while attending a university there. She uses canna leaves to make the packets, but if you can't find them, substitute banana leaves, which can be found in Latin and Asian markets.

8	eggs, separated	½	teaspoon ground anise seed
1⅛	cups sugar	2	tablespoons water
1	cup butter	1	cup raisins
4	cups white corn flour (masa harina)	6	canna leaf sections, about 6- by 6-inches
1	cup milk		

Beat the egg yolks with the sugar and butter until creamy. Add the flour and milk alternately, stirring well. Add the anise seed and water and stir. Beat the egg whites until stiff and fold into the batter. Add the raisins and stir.

Wrap the batter in the banana leaf sections, folding the leaves so they make packets. Tie the packets with string and place in a steamer, or in the top of a double boiler. Steam, covered, for 20 minutes.

Yield: 6 servings

Platanos con Crema Natilla

(Cinnamon-Spiced Plantains with Natilla Cream)

This recipe was given to *Chile Pepper* food editor Nancy Gerlach by Melena, her Costa Rican guide on an expedition to the habanero fields at Los Chiles. Plantains are a staple in the Costa Rican diet and are served at any meal. Bananas can be substituted if plantains are not available, and the combination of creams is a substitute for one found in Costa Rica.

2	tablespoons butter	3	tablespoons heavy cream
1	tablespoon honey	4	tablespoons sour cream
¼	teaspoon ground cinnamon		
2	large plantains or bananas, peeled and sliced lengthwise		

Melt the butter in a skillet and stir in the honey and cinnamon. Fry the plantains in the mixture until soft, turning once. Combine the two creams and mix well.

Place the plantains on plates, pour some of the honey-cinnamon mixture over them, top with the cream mixture, and serve.

Yield: 2 servings

Torta de Coco com Frutas
(Coconut Pie with Tropical Fruits)

This Brazilian version of coconut pie is topped with your selection of tropical fruits. We have made a few suggestions, but feel free to explore your Latin market for other possibilities.

1 9-inch prepared unbaked pie shell
2 cups milk
4 eggs
½ cup sugar
¼ teaspoon salt
½ teaspoon vanilla

2 tablespoons butter
½ cup freshly grated coconut
 Slices of fresh mango, papaya, guava, and banana, cut into the shapes of stars and quarter moons for garnish

Chill the pie shell for 30 minutes before baking. Preheat the oven to 350°F.

Scald the milk in a double boiler until bubbles form around the outer edge of the pan. Beat the eggs in a bowl and add the sugar, salt, vanilla, butter, and grated coconut. Stir in the scalded milk and transfer the mixture to the pie shell.

Bake for about 30 minutes or until the custard is set. Remove from the heat, let cool, and transfer to the refrigerator.

Cut the pie and decorate each piece with the carved fruits.

Yield: 6 to 8 servings

Pastel de Almendras y Mango

(Almond and Mango Pie)

This Guatemalan delight is deceptively easy to make, considering its fabulous taste. North Americans don't have too many choices when selecting mangoes, but we can recommend two varieties to look for: the pale yellow "Manila" and the incredibly textured "Julie."

1	15-ounce can condensed milk
6	large mangoes, peeled, pitted, and coarsely chopped
3	eggs, separated, whites beaten until stiff with 1 tablespoon sugar

⅓	cup ground almonds
1	9-inch baked pie shell, cooled
3	teaspoons sugar
	Ground allspice (*pimento*) for garnish

In a blender, combine the condensed milk, mangoes, egg yolks, and almonds. Blend briefly until a thick mixture forms, but do not puree fine.

Transfer to the baked pie shell. In a bowl, combine the egg whites and the sugar and spread over the mango mixture. Bake at 350°F until golden brown, about 30 minutes.

Remove the pie from the oven, cool on a wire rack, sprinkle the allspice over the pie, and serve.

Yield: 6 to 8 servings

Pastel de Platanos y Nogadas

(Banana and Walnut Pie)

Our final pie, from Venezuela, features tropical bananas and walnuts. We recommend the small finger bananas in this recipe (use 12), but the standard Cavendish variety will work.

6 ripe bananas	¼ teaspoon nutmeg
½ cup sugar	½ teaspoon powdered ginger
1 tablespoon melted butter	3 egg whites, beaten until stiff
½ cup ground walnuts	1 9-inch prepared unbaked pie shell
1 cup seedless raisins	
1 teaspoon powdered allspice	Powdered allspice for garnish

Preheat the oven to 425°F.

Mash the bananas until smooth. Add the sugar, butter, walnuts, raisins, allspice, nutmeg, and ginger and mix well. Fold in the egg whites.

Transfer the mixture to the pie shell and bake for 30 minutes. Remove the pie from the oven, sprinkle the allspice over it, and cool before serving. ·

Yield: 8 servings

We Thought the Latin Translated as "Wisdom of the Muse"

"Banana is a Portuguese word for a fruit known throughout history. The original food for thought, its botanical name is *Musa sapientum*, 'the man who thinks,' said to come from the legend of wise men who sat under the shade of the tree, eating bananas. The banana is an herb, not a tree." —Martin Elkhort

Bolo de Nozes com Vinho

(Brazil Nut Wine Cake)

Again, alcohol is added to a Latin American dessert. And this one features the Brazil nut, one of the few food crops that is not cultivated, but is harvested in the wild from pods. One food historian wrote, "If one of these immense woody pods fall from the heights of the Amazon's 150-foot trees onto the head of an incautious gatherer, it can split his skull asunder."

4	cups sugar	½	teaspoon salt
1	cup butter	2	teaspoons powdered cocoa
12	eggs, separated, yolks lightly beaten; 6 whites beaten until stiff	1	teaspoon ground cinnamon
		2	cups milk
4	cups sifted flour	½	cup port wine
1	tablespoon baking powder	2	cups finely chopped Brazil nuts

Combine the sugar and butter and beat until creamy. Add the egg yolks and beat well. Sift together the flour, baking powder, salt, cocoa, and cinnamon and add to the egg mixture. Add the milk, wine, and Brazil nuts and mix well. Fold in the egg whites.

Bake in a greased and floured 10-inch tube pan for 1 hour at 375°F, checking after about 45 minutes to make sure it isn't browning too much or burning. Turn the temperature down to 350°F for the final 15 minutes.

Yield: 15 servings

Tortas de Cacao

(Colombian Cocoa Cakes)

Chocolate, that uniquely New World dessert flavoring, makes its appearance in these little cakes. Serve them with your favorite ice cream—or be daring—serve them with our Gelado de Abacate (Avocado Ice Cream, p. 256.

½	cup butter	1	tablespoon baking powder
1	cup sugar		Pinch of salt
3	eggs	⅔	cup milk
¾	cup powdered cocoa	1	teaspoon vanilla
1½ cups flour			

Preheat the oven to 375°F.

Beat the butter until creamy, add the sugar, and continue to beat until the mixture is light and fluffy. Add the eggs, one at a time, beating well each time.

Sift together the cocoa, flour, baking powder, and salt. Add the dry ingredients and the milk to the egg mixture and beat until smooth. Add the vanilla and beat well.

Transfer the batter to greased and floured muffin tins, filling each cup ⅔ full. Bake the tins for 20 minutes until a cake tester comes out clean.

Remove the cakes from the tins and cool on wire racks.

Yield: About 16 cakes

Torta Criolla de Queso

(Creole Passion Fruit Cheesecake)

Our Venezuelan cheesecake features the flavor of the Latin American passion fruit. Dave enjoyed his first taste of this tropical fruit on Marie Sharp's veranda in the citrus plantations of Belize's Maya Mountains, where Marie served passion fruit drinks to him and Nancy and Jeff Gerlach.

8 eggs, separated; whites beaten until stiff

1 cup sugar

1 pound cream cheese, at room temperature

1 teaspoon baking powder

¼ cup passion fruit juice

Preheat the oven to 350°F.

Beat the egg yolks and sugar together until thick. Beat in the cream cheese until the mixture is smooth. Add the baking powder, stir, and fold in the egg whites and passion fruit juice.

Transfer the mixture to a buttered, 8-inch springform pan and bake for 45 minutes.

Yield: 8–10 servings

Torta de Pasa

(Raisin Cake)

Wherever grapes are grown, raisins are produced as well, and this holds true for Paraguay, where the raisins are used in desserts such as this cake.

¾ cup sugar

½ cup water

1   tablespoon cornstarch

1   cup seedless raisins

½ cup chopped pecans

½ cup butter

½ cup dark brown sugar

2   eggs, beaten

2   cups flour

1½ teaspoons cream of tartar

1½ teaspoons baking soda

½ cup milk

1   teaspoon vanilla

Preheat the oven to 350°F.

Combine one-half cup of the sugar, the water, and cornstarch in a saucepan, mix well, and cook over low heat until the mixture thickens, about 5 minutes. Remove from the heat, add the raisins and pecans, and set aside.

Beat the butter until soft, add the remaining sugar and the brown sugar and beat until smooth. Add the eggs and beat well.

Sift together the flour, cream of tartar, and baking soda and add to the butter mixture along with the milk and vanilla. Beat well until a smooth batter forms.

Spoon half of this batter into a greased 8-inch square pan. Spread the raisin-pecan mixture over the batter and cover with the remaining batter.

Bake for 40 minutes or until a cake tester comes out clean.

Yield: 8 servings

Mail-Order Sources

Many of the ingredients mentioned in the recipes are carried by the companies listed below.

Chile Pepper Magazine
P.O. Box 80780
Albuquerque, NM 87198
(800) 359-1483

The magazine of spicy world cuisine.

Colorado Spice Company
5030 Nome St., Unit A
Denver, CO 80239
(303) 373-0141

Spices, herbs, and chile peppers.

Dean and DeLuca
Mail Order Department
560 Broadway
New York, NY 10012
(212) 431-1691

Exotic herbs and spices from around the world.

Don Alfonso Foods
P.O. Box 201988
Austin, TX 78720
(800) 456-6100

Imported Mexican and Latin American chiles; chipotles in adobo in glass containers.

Enchanted Seeds
P.O. Box 6087
Las Cruces, NM 88006
(505) 233-3033

Exotic chile seeds, including habanero, ají, and rocoto.

Frieda's, Inc.
4465 Corporate Center Dr.
Los Alamitos, CA 90720-2561
(800) 241-1771

Fresh and dried habaneros and other exotic chiles.

G. B. Ratto & Co.
821 Washington St.
Oakland, CA 94607
(510) 836-2250

Exotic spices and foods from all over the world.

Le Saucier
Faneuil Hall Marketplace
Boston, MA 02109
(617) 227-9649

Sauces, salsas, and condiments from all over the world.

Los Dos, Inc.
P.O. Box 7548
Albuquerque, NM 87194
(505) 831-9161

Distributor of Rica Red habanero
products.

Melissa's World Variety Produce
P.O. Box 21127
Los Angeles, CA 90021
(800) 468-7111

Fresh, dried, and pickled habaneros.

Nancy's Specialty Market
P.O. Box 327
Wye Mills, MD 21679
(800) 462-6291

Spices, herbs, hot sauces, coconut
extract, coconut milk, curry pastes,
Indian pickles and chutneys.

Old Southwest Trading Company
P.O. Box 7545
Albuquerque, NM 87194
(505) 836-0168

New Mexican and Mexican chiles; Latin
sauces and salsas.

Pepper Gal
P.O. Box 23006
Ft. Lauderdale, FL 33307
(305) 537-5540

Habanero and other exotic chile seeds.

Seed Savers Exchange
Rt. 3, Box 239
Decorah, IA 52101

Seed Savers Exchange is dedicated to
the preservation of heirloom seed varieties, including many habaneros, rocotos, and ajís. They publish an annual
yearbook listing available varieties.

Shepherd's Garden Seeds
6116 Highway 9
Felton, CA 95108
(408) 335-5216

Latin chile peppers and exotic vegetable
seeds.

Stonewall Chile Pepper Company
P.O. Box 241
Stonewall, TX 78671
(800) 232-2995

Habanero products, including pods and
salsas.

USDA-ARS Plant Introduction Station
1109 Experiment St.
Griffin, GA 30223-1797

The public may request seeds of certain
habanero, ajís, and rocotos. Include
SASE with request.

Glossary

Note: Many of the ingredients in the following list are available in Latin, Caribbean, and Asian markets.

achiote: the orange-colored seeds of the annatto tree; used as a coloring agent and seasoning. Also called annato.

aguacate: avocado; *abacate* in Brazil

aguas frescas: fresh fruit drinks

ají: the common name for chiles in Latin America; usually *Capsicum baccatum*

ajo: garlic

albóndigas: meatballs

al carbón: charcoal grilled

al pastór: cooked on a spit over a fire

almuerzo: lunch

ananá: pineapple

ancho chile: a wide, dark, mild Mexican chile with a raisin-like aroma and flavor

annuum: the species of chile that includes the jalapeño and most familiar Mexican and American varieties

anticuchos: charbroiled beef hearts on skewers

antojito: literally, "little whim"; an appetizer

arroz: rice

asada or **asado:** roasted or broiled

azafran: saffron

bacalhau: salt cod

baccatum: the species of chiles that includes the South American ajís

batida: a blended drink

biftec or **bistec:** beef

borracho: literally, "drunken"; foods containing beer or liquor

cachaça: a Brazilian rum

calabacita: squash, usually zucchini-types

calamari: squid

caldo: a broth, stock, or clear soup

camarão or **camarón:** shrimp

camote: sweet potato

cancha: toasted corn

canela: cinnamon

caipirinha: a Brazilian cocktail made with *cachaça*

cancha: toasted corn served over Peruvian ceviche

carne: meat

carne seca: jerky

cassareep: the boiled down juice of manioc

cassava: a tropical root that is the source of tapioca; also called manioc and *yuca*

cazuela: a pottery cooking dish or the stew cooked in one; a Chilean stew

cebolla: onion

cena: dinner

cerdo: pork

ceviche: raw seafood combined with citrus juice, which "cooks" the fish by combining with its protein and turning it opaque

chala: Argentinian expression for corn husk

chancho: South American term for pig or pork

chayote: a pear-shaped squash

chicha: a beer made from corn

chicharrones: fried pork skins; also, spare ribs

chile: referring to the plants or pods of the *Capsicum* genus

chinense: the species of chiles that includes the habanero

chipotle: literally, any smoked chile; usually refers to smoked jalapeños

chorizo: a spicy sausage made with pork, garlic, and red chile powder

chuño: freeze-dried potatoes

chupe: a Peruvian stew or chowder

churrasco: barbecued meat

cilantro: an annual herb (*Coriandrum sativum*) with seeds that are known as

coriander. Substitute: Italian parsley, or *culantro (Eryngium foetidum)*. Commonly used in salsas and soups

cobán chile: a smoked Guatemalan piquin chile; substitute *chipotle*

cochayuyo: a Peruvian sea vegetable

cocina: kitchen; cuisine

coco: coconut

comino or **cumin:** an annual herb (*Cuminum cyminum*) whose seeds have a distinctive odor

cozido: a Brazilian stew

cuy: guinea pig; also, *cui*

dende: palm oil

desayuno: breakfast

empadinha: a Brazilian pastry turnover

empanada: a pastry turnover

empanadita: a small pastry turnover

enchiladas: rolled or stacked corn tortillas filled with meat or cheese and covered with chile sauce

ensalada: salad

epazote: known as "Ambrosia" in English, this perennial herb (*Chenopodium ambrosioides*) is strong and bitter and is used primarily to flavor beans

escabeche: foods marinated or pickled in vinegar

farofa: a Brazilian condiment made with manioc flour and often hot chiles

feijoada: a Brazilian dish of rice, beans, and meat

flan: a baked caramel custard dessert

frijoles: beans

frutescens: the species of chiles that include the tabasco

gallina: hen

gallo: rooster

gallo pinto: beans and rice, the favorite dish of Costa Rica

golosinas: sweets

guasacaca: a Venezuelan barbecue sauce

guisado: stew

habanero chiles: literally, "from Havana"; small orange or red chiles from South America, the Caribbean, and Yucatán that resemble a tam or bonnet; *Capsicum chinense,* the hottest pepper in the world

hervido: a Venezuelan stew

hongos: mushrooms

huachinango: red snapper

huevos: eggs

humitas: stuffed corn husks

jamón: ham

jícama: a white tuber *(Pachyrhizus erosus)* used in salads and tastes like a cross between an apple and a potato

jocón: a Guatemalan stewed chicken

lengua: tongue

lima: lemon

limón: lime

llapingachos: potato-cheese cakes

locro: a thick stew

lomo: loin

maíz: corn

malagueta: *Capsicum frutescens,* a Brazilian chile related to tabascos

manteca: lard

marisco: shellfish

masa: corn dough

masa harina: corn flour

matambre: literally, "kill hunger," an Argentinian meat dish

maté: a Paraguayan tea made from the leaves of *Hilea paraguaiensis,* a species of holly tree

melegueta pepper: a spicy African berry *(Aframomum melegueta)* not related to *Capsicums*

mole: thick chile sauces with many ingredients that are popular in Mexico and northern Central America

môlho: a Brazilian sauce

moqueca: a fish stew from Bahia, Brazil

naranja: orange

nopales or **nopalitos:** prickly pear cactus pods, spines removed

nueces: walnuts

ocopa: a Peruvian hot sauce served over potatoes

olla: a round, earthenware pot

ostra: oyster

palillo: a Peruvian herb that imparts a yellow hue to foods

palta: South American term for avocado

pan: bread

pan dulce: sweet bread

papas: potatoes

papa seca: dried potatoes

parrilla: grill or broiler

pasa: raisin

pasilla: a long, thin, mild, dark Mexican chile that is used in *mole* sauces

pastel: a pastry turnover; pie

pato: duck

pavo: turkey

pepitas: squash or pumpkin seeds

pescado: fish

picadillo: shredded beef, spices, and other ingredients usually used as a stuffing

picante: hot and spicy

piña: pineapple

piquin: a small, very hot chile grown all over the Americas; usually used in dry form

Pisco: Peruvian brandy

pollo: chicken

pimento: allspice

pimiento: the familiar, olive-stuffing pepper

pubescens: the species of chiles that includes the South American rocotos

puchero: a stew in Argentina, Uruguay, Paraguay, and Bolivia

puerco: pork

queso: cheese

queso blanco: white cheese

quinoa: (pronounced *keen-wah*) an Andean grain

rajas: strips; usually refers to strips of chiles

relleno: stuffed

repollo, repôlho: cabbage

res: beef

ristra: a string of red chile pods

rocoto: the round, thick-walled chiles of the Andes; *Capsicum pubescens*

salsa: literally, "sauce," but usually used to describe uncooked sauces (*salsa cruda*)

salteña: a pastry turnover from Bolivia

sancochado: a Peruvian stew

sancocho: a stew in Ecuador and Colombia

sopa: soup

tamal: (plural, tamales), any filling enclosed in masa, wrapped in a corn husk, and steamed

tamarindo: tamarind

torta: tart, cake, and sometimes pie

vatapá: a Brazilian shrimp dish

yerba buena: mint

Bibliography

Alzugaray, Domingo and Catia (eds.)
   1984. *Enciclopedia da Flora Brasileira*. São Paulo, Brazil: Tres Livros e Fasciculos.

Andrews, Jean
   1984. *Peppers: The Domesticated Capsicums*. Austin: University of Texas Press.
   1988. "Around the World with the Chili Pepper: Post Colombian Distribution of Domesticated Capsicums." *Journal of Gastronomy,* Vol. 4, No. 3 (Autumn), 21.
   1993. *Red Hot Peppers*. New York: Macmillan.

Baker, Charles H.
   1951. *The South American Gentleman's Companion*. New York: Crown Publishers.

Barbarek, Bernard
   1982. *The Best Recipes from 20 Hispanic Countries*. Springfield, MO: Nuevos Horizontes.

Barty-King, Hugh and Anton Massel
   1983. *Rum Yesterday and Today*. London: William Heinemann Ltd.

Baudin, Louis
   1968. *Daily Life in Peru Under the Last Incas*. New York: The Macmillan Company.

Beals, Carleton
   1961. *Nomads and Empire Builders: Native Peoples and Cultures of South America*. Philadelphia: Chilton Company.

Benson, Elizabeth P.
   1967. *The Maya World*. New York: Thomas Y. Crowell Co.

Bensusan, Susan
   1973. *Latin American Cooking*. New York: Galahad Books.

Botafogo, Dolores
   1960. *The Art of Brazilian Cookery*. New York: Doubleday & Co.

Brothwell, Dan and Patricia
    1969. *Food in Antiquity.* London: Thames and Hudson.

Brown, Cora, Rose, and Bob
    1939. *The South American Cook Book.* New York: Doubleday, Doran & Co. (Reprint, New York: Dover, 1971).

Coady, Chantal
    1993. *Chocolate, The Food of the Gods.* San Francisco: Chronicle Books.

Cobo, Father Bernabe
    1979. *History of the Inca Empire.* Austin: University of Texas Press.

Coe, Sophie D.
    1994. *America's First Cuisines.* Austin: University of Texas Press.

Conce, Na
    1951. *Creole Cookery: The Art of Cooking Peruvian Food.* Lima: Talleres Graficos.

de la Vega, Garcilaso (El Inca)
    1966. *Royal Commentaries of the Incas.* Trans. Harold V. Livermore from the 1609 work. Austin: University of Texas Press.

Dempsey, Mary
    1991. "Will Kill a Gringo: Fiery Peruvian Food." *Chile Pepper*, Nov.–Dec.

Descola, Jean
    1968. *Daily Life in Colonial Peru, 1710–1820.* New York: The Macmillan Company.

DeWitt, Dave and Paul Bosland
    1993. *The Pepper Garden.* Berkeley: Ten Speed Press.

DeWitt, Dave and Nancy Gerlach
    1989. "Expedition to Belize." *Chile Pepper*, Summer, 38.

    1990. *The Whole Chile Pepper Book.* Boston: Little, Brown.

    1993. "Quest for Fire: In Search of Hot Stuff in Costa Rica." *Chile Pepper*, July–Aug.

Elkhort, Martin
    1991. *The Secret Life of Food.* Los Angeles: Jeremy P. Tarcher, Inc.

Fussell, Betty
    1992. *The Story of Corn.* New York: Alfred A. Knopf.

Galarza, Winifred
    1994. Interview with Mary Jane Wilan, June 12.

Galeano, Eduardo
    1985. *Memory of Fire: 1. Genesis.* New York: Pantheon Books.

Gheerbrant, Alain
    1992. *The Amazon Past, Present, and Future*. New York: Harry N. Abrams.

Harris, Jessica B.
    1985. *Hot Stuff*. New York: Ballantine Books.
    1992. *Tasting Brazil*. New York: Macmillan.

Hawkes, Alex D.
    1978. *The Flavors of the Caribbean and Latin America*. New York: The Viking Press.

Hazen-Hammond, Susan
    1994. "The Search for the Bad-Word Chile." *Chile Pepper*, July–Aug.

Herbst, Sharon Tyler
    1990. *Food Lover's Companion*. New York: Barron's.

Humboldt, Alexander von
    1852. *Personal Narrative of Travels to the Equinoctial Regions of America During the Years 1799–1804*. London & New York: George Routledge and Sons.

Karoff, Barbara
    1989. *South American Cooking*. Berkeley: Aris Books.

Kaufman, William I.
    1964. *The Wonderful World of Cooking: Recipes from the Caribbean and Latin America*. New York: Dell.

Kelly, Brian and Mark London
    1983. *Amazon*. New York: Harcourt Brace Jovanovich.

Koock, Mary Faulk
    1967. *Cuisine of the Americas*. Austin: Cookbook Associates.

Lackey, Maria (ed.)
    1960. *Pan-American Cook Book*. Buenos Aires: American Women's Club of Buenos Aires.

Leonard, Jonathan Norton
    1968. *Latin American Cooking*. New York: Time-Life Books.
    1968. *Recipes: Latin American Cooking*. New York: Time-Life Books.

Libín, Tita
    1994. "The Voodoo Foods of Bahia." *Chile Pepper*, July–Aug.

Lichine, Alexis
    1968. *Alexis Lichine's Encyclopedia of Wines & Spirits*. New York: Alfred A. Knopf.

Marks, Copeland
1985. *False Tongues and Sunday Bread: A Guatemalan and Mayan Cookbook.* New York: M. Evans.

Mars, W. B. and Carlos Rizzini
1966. *Useful Plants of Brazil.* San Francisco: Holden-Day, Inc.

Murua, M. de
1962. *Historia General de Perú, Origen y Descendencia de Los Incas.* Madrid: Biblioteca Americana Vetus.

Nagai, H.
1989. "Tomato and Pepper Production in Brazil." In *Tomato and Pepper Production in the Tropics,* ed. by T. D. Griggs and B. T. McLean. Taipei, Taiwan: Asian Vegetable Research and Development Center.

Naj, Amal
1992. *Peppers: A Story of Hot Pursuits.* New York: Knopf.

Ortiz, Elisabeth (ed.)
1991. *Book of Latin American Cooking.* London: Penguin.
1992. *The Encyclopedia of Herbs, Spices & Flavorings.* London: Dorling Kindersley, Inc.
1992. *A Little Brazilian Cookbook.* San Francisco: Chronicle Books.

Oviedo, Gonzalo Fernándo de
1985. "Della Naturale e Generale Istoria dell'Indie." In Giovanni Batista Ramusio, *Navigazione e Viaggi,* Vol. 5. Torino: Einaudi.

Parrish, David
1994. "Ecuador: Land of Ají." *Chile Pepper,* July–Aug.

Pickersgill, Barbara
1969. "The Archaeological Record of Chili Peppers (Capsicum spp.) and the Sequence of Plant Domestication in Peru." *American Antiquity,* Vol. 34, No. 1, 54–61.

Rojas-Lombardi, Felipe
1991. *The Art of South American Cooking.* New York: HarperCollins.

Schumann, Charles
1989. *Tropical Bar Book.* New York: Stewart, Tabori and Chang.

Schwabe, Calvin W.
1979. *Unmentionable Cuisine.* Charlottesville: University Press of Virginia.

Scott, David and Eve Bletcher
1994. *Latin American Vegetarian Cookery.* London: Rider.

Sokolov, Raymond
1990. "Soul Food in the New World." *Natural History,* Aug., 74.

Super, John C.
1988. *Food, Conquest, and Colonization in Sixteenth Century Spanish America.* Albuquerque: University of New Mexico Press.

Tume, Lynelle
1979. *Latin American Cookbook.* London: Tiger Books International.

Valcárcel, L. E.
1925. *Del Ayllu al Imperio.* Lima, Peru.

Van Harten, A. M.
1970. "Melegueta Pepper." *Economic Botany,* Vol. 24, 208.

Verrill, A. Hyatt
1937. *Foods America Gave the World.* Boston: L. C. Page & Co.

Vietmeyer, Noel D. (ed.)
1989. *Lost Crops of the Incas.* Washington, D.C.: National Academy Press.

Von Hagen, Victor W.
1957. *Realm of the Incas.* New York: Mentor Books.

Waldo, Myra
1961. *The Art of South American Cookery.* New York: Doubleday & Co.

Wasson, Betty
1962. *Cooks, Gluttons & Gourmets: A History of Cookery.* New York: Doubleday & Co.

Whitlock, Ralph
1976. *Everyday Life of the Maya.* New York: Dorset Press.

Index